How to care for
more Flowering
Houseplants

Series editor: David Longman

Colour illustrations by Jane Fern and Josephine Martin

How to care for
more Flowering
Houseplants

y Tom Gough

Peter Lowe

THE AUTHOR

Tom Gough trained in horticulture with the famous
houseplant growers, Thomas Rochford, and studied floristry
both in Britain and the Netherlands. He is a liveryman of The
Worshipful Company of Gardeners, a past chairman of the
London district of Interflora and a director of Longmans the
Florist in London.

Printed in Italy by Amilcare Pizzi SpA

Contents

Common names

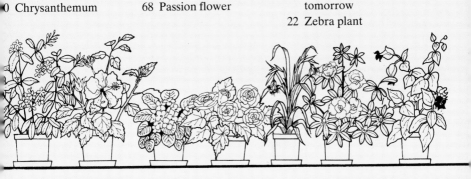

Scientific names

Introduction

How to use this book

How often have you bought or been given a beautiful flowering plant, only to find that after a week or so it looks decidedly past its best and you have no idea how to prolong its life? This book, one of two volumes on flowering houseplants in a comprehensive houseplant series, is here to help with really practical advice.

It describes the flowering houseplants that you are likely to find in shops, garden centres – even motorway service stations. Each plant has a self-contained two-page entry. On the left is a general description of the plant with details of how to look after it, giving the correct amounts of water, light, warmth and humidity it needs, explaining how to clean and repot it and when and if it needs pruning. There is also a colour photo of a healthy leaf or flower. On the right-hand page is a colour illustration of the plant showing all the things that can go wrong with it. Since this picture shows all the troubles at once, some of the plants look very sick indeed! To find out what is wrong with your plant, look for its symptoms in the illustration. Read the caption next to the part of the picture that shows the same features as your plant. It tells you what is wrong and how to put it right.

Different plants require different conditions and it is important to know each one's special requirements. Chrysanthemums, for example, soon die in hot rooms; azaleas need a cool temperature and copious amounts of soft water. Most flowering plants need more light than other houseplants if they are to produce a good crop of flowers but not all require high temperatures and many must actually be shaded from direct sunlight. So whether you are beginning with a familiar African violet or progressing to an exotic Slipper orchid, make sure you read the detailed care instructions for your plant and you will be able to look after it with confidence.

Tools for indoor gardening

It is possible to look after plants with the minimum of equip – a watering can, sprayer and plastic sponge are the real essentials. However, for long-term houseplant care, you wi need a much more comprehensive collection, which can be acquired gradually as the need arises.

Keep separate sprayers and watering cans for insecticides and fungicides and a stock of basic insecticides. Methylated spirits is useful for removing some pests. Mark all containers used for insecticides clearly and wash them out regularly.

Most flowering plants react badly to leafshine and should be cleaned with a fine mist spray or with a damp sponge or soft cloth. For delicate leaves use a feather duster or dry paintbrush. A paintbrush and cotton-wool are useful for removing pests.

A small garden trowel and fork are useful when repotting or adding topsoil. A large spoon is a good substitute. A plastic bucket is essential for mixing composts, wetting peat and for giving very dry plants a thorough soaking.

Keep a selection of loam-based and peat-based composts, some pure moss or sedge peat. Some plants require lime-free mixtures. Sharp sand can be obtained from garden centres. Fertilizer, hormone rooting powder and charcoal are all useful.

Two watering cans to which a rose can be attached are useful, one pint (½ litre) size, the other holding about a gallon (4½l). Never use your normal watering can for insecticides or fungicides.

Scissors, secateurs and a sharp knife are useful for removing dead or damaged leaves.

Keep a small stock of flower pots and saucers, both plastic and clay. Old clay flower pots can be broken up to make excellent drainage material. Outer pots, with no drainage holes, can be used to hide the standard pot.

Twine, string, raffia and plant rings are essential for climbing plants, with a selection of canes, sticks and moss poles.

Watering and spraying

More houseplants are killed by incorrect watering (mainly of the little and often variety) than by anything else. Most prefer to be given a good soaking, then left almost to dry out before they are watered again. Some must be kept always moist – but in these cases the pot must be well drained so that the roots do not become waterlogged. Others prefer to dry out more thoroughly between waterings. Some need more water at one time of year than another. Always test the compost before watering to see how dry it is below the surface. In cold weather do not use cold water straight from the tap or the shock may damage the plant. Use tepid water for both watering and spraying.

Spraying keeps a plant's leaves clean and also provides extra humidity in hot, dry rooms. Avoid tap water if possible as the lime it contains clogs the pores of the leaves. Rainwater collected in a tank or bucket, water from melted ice in the freezer or boiled water which has been allowed to cool are all more suitable. Do not spray in bright sunlight as the water acts like a magnifying glass and may cause burn or scorch marks. A few plants dislike water on their leaves so before spraying you should check the individual requirements under each plant entry. Most, however benefit from a fine mist spray.

Feeding

Most composts contain fertilizer but for healthy growth plants also need extra nourishment, usually in spring and summer. Houseplant food or fertilizer is available as a liquid, diluted before use, as a powder added to water, as granules scattered on the surface of the soil and as a pill or stick pushed into the soil and gradually absorbed. For most houseplants a liquid food is most suitable. It is clean, has no smell, and is easy and economical to use. There are several brands available and it is a good idea to try several and to change from time to time. Normally you can simply follow the instructions on the bottle, adding a few drops to the water in the can when watering.

Watering

1. Test compost for dryness with finger or knife blade before watering. If blade comes out clean or soil dry and crumbly, compost is drying out. If soil sticks, it is still moist. Check instructions for each plant: some like a dry interval, others must be always moist.

2. Add water to top of compost, filling pot to the brim. Excess water will drain into saucer. After 15 minutes, empty any water remaining in the saucer. Do not allow pot to stand in water.

3. If plant is very dried out and does not mind water on its leaves, plunge pot into bowl so that water covers pot rim. Spray leaves. Leave for 15 minutes, then take it out and allow it to drain.

4. If plant cannot tolerate water on its leaves, add water to fill the saucer and wait for at least 15 minutes for it to be absorbed. Empty excess so plant does not stand in water. Or, plunge pot into bowl or bucket of water to just below pot rim. Leave for 15 minutes, then take out and allow to drain.

5. Bromeliads such as the Scarlet star *(Guzmania)* need to have water in their central well. Use rainwater if possible and fill whenever watering compost.

Cleaning the leaves
1. Flick very dusty plants with a feather duster before cleaning. Be careful not to damage leaves or flowers.

2. Wipe larger leaves with a damp cloth or sponge to remove dust and any insects such as red spider mite. Use soft water if possible. Remember to wipe the undersides of the leaves as well as the tops.

3. Spraying (with soft water if possible) is often enough to keep plants clean. The lime in hard tap water may mark the leaves and clog the pores. Do not spray the flowers and do not spray in sunlight.

4. Very few flowering plants tolerate leafshine on their leaves as they are easily burned or clogged by the oils it contains. Check instructions and never use more than once a month.

Humidity

Some flowering plants require higher humidity than is found in normal rooms, especially in dry, centrally heated homes. A group of plants will create its own more humid atmosphere but you can improve the humidity around them in several ways.

1. Spray regularly with soft water, holding spray about 6in (15cm) from plant. Do not spray in strong sunlight. Spray may mark or rot flowers, so check plant's requirements.

2. Put pebbles in plant's saucer and stand pot on top. Add water to saucer until it comes half way up the pebbles. Do not let bottom of pot touch water or plant will become waterlogged and roots will rot away. Water vapour will rise from the damp pebbles, providing extra humidity, under the leaves. Add more water to saucer when pebbles begin to dry. A group of plants can be placed together on a tray of damp pebbles for even better local humidity.

3. Place pot inside a larger container and pack the space between the two with damp peat. Keep peat constantly moist. This is a good method to use if you have to leave the plants for some time as the peat will hold moisture well.

Pruning

Old flowering plants may grow straggly and produce fewer flowers. Pruning back leggy stems in spring encourages new side shoots which in turn produce more flowers. In general, cut stems down by half, just above a leaf or side shoot. But read individual instructions.

Cut off dead flowers so that plant's energy goes to new buds and leaves.

For some plants, however, the mixture must be weaker than the manufacturer recommends on the bottle. If it is used at too concentrated a strength, it will damage the roots. Never increase the recommended strength and be careful with tablets and fertilizer sticks. If they are too close to the roots, the concentrated fertilizer may cause root damage

If in doubt, don't feed. It is always better to slightly underfeed than to overfeed – and never feed a sick plant.

Repotting

Plants need repotting either because the roots have totally filled the existing pot and can no longer develop or because the nutritional value of the compost has been used up. It's quite easy to tell if a plant needs repotting. Remove it from its pot (see right). If there is a mass of roots and no soil showing, it needs repotting – it is potbound. If any soil is visible, don't repot. Replace plant in its old pot and gently firm it back in position. Other signs are roots growing through the pot base and weak, slow growth. Newly purchased plants should not normally need repotting. Do not repot unhealthy plants: the shock may kill them. In fact if in doubt, don't repot.

Repotting is usually done in spring – March or April in the northern hemisphere, September or October in the southern, but some winter-flowering plants are repotted in early autumn. Most plants require good drainage so that water can run through the compost freely and air can get to the roots. Broken crocks from old clay flower pots or a layer of coarse gravel at the bottom of the pot will provide drainage. Never use a container without drainage holes in its base. Put a piece of paper or a layer of moss over the drainage crocks to stop the compost from blocking the holes and inspect the root ball for pests. Remove old stones, damaged roots and old soil and gently remove old, loose compost from the top to a depth of about ½in (1cm). Then place plant in new pot.

After repotting, leave the plant without water for 2–3 days. The roots will spread out into the new compost in search of water. If it is very hot, spray the leaves every day.

Choosing the right compost: The correct type of compost or soil is very important for indoor plants. Don't use garden soil. Compost types vary considerably as some house plants need a very light peat-based compost and some a heavy loam. The correct combination for each plant is given in the individual entries.

The two most commonly used types of compost are loam-based or peat-based. Loam-based compost is made up of sterilized loam (soil) mixed with peat and grit or coarse, washed sand. It is usually sold with fertilizer added, following formulae developed by the John Innes Institute for Horticultural Research. The numbers 1, 2 and 3 indicate the different proportions of fertilizer added. In this book they are referred to as 'loam-based No. 1, 2 or 3'.

Peat-based composts are more open in texture, sterile, and hold moisture longer. They are normally composed of 10 parts of peat to 1 part of coarse sand with fertilizer added in the same proportions as loam-based compost. It is important when using peat composts not to firm them into the pot too hard. Plants absorb the fertilizer content more quickly from these composts than from loam-based ones.

Ericaceous or lime-free compost is available for plants that do not tolerate lime such as Gardenias. Sphagnum moss is useful for mixing in special composts or for lining a hanging basket. Sharp sand is fine washed sand, available from garden centres. Do not use coarse builders' sand. Sharp sand is sometimes mixed with loam to give a specially well-drained compost for plants that need frequent, copious watering.

Mixing compost: If mixing your own blend of compost, put the different items into a plastic bucket, using the same measure for each one. A plant pot or old cup will do. For 2 parts loam, 1 part peat, for example, fill the measure twice with loam, then once with peat. Mix the items together well with trowel or stick.

Taking cuttings

This is the most common way of propagating houseplants though seeds of some species are available. First prepare a small pot with drainage and special rooting compost.

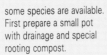

3. Dust the cut ends with hormone rooting powder.

5. Place in heated propagator or cover with polythene and keep in warm place (70°F, 21°C). Keep watered and remove cover for 5 minutes a day.

6. When cuttings begin to grow (in about 4 weeks), pot singly in small pots,

1. Choose a healthy stem tip or side stem and cut off the top 3–4in (8–10cm). Cuttings should include a growing tip and 2 pairs of healthy leaves.

2. Remove lowest pair of leaves and any side shoots from bottom part so there is a length of bare stem to insert into compost. Prepare other cuttings in the same way.

4. Make holes around edge of new pot. Insert several cuttings and firm compost gently round them. Water well.

Repotting

Offsets

Bromeliads such as Scarlet star *(Guzmania lingulata)* produce offsets which can be separated from the parent plant when they are about half its size and have their own root system.

1. Prepare clean, dry pot not more than 2 sizes larger than old one. Place broken crocks or coarse gravel in bottom as drainage, then a piece of paper or moss and layer of new compost. Water plant well.

3. Remove damaged or dead roots with sharp knife.

5. Lower plant into new pot and add more compost round root ball, firming it with fingers or a round stick. Continue adding compost until pot is filled to within ½–¾in (1–1½cm). Leave without water in shade for 3 days.

1. Remove offset and roots from parent plant with sharp knife.

2. Hold pot upside down as shown. Gently tap rim of pot on edge of table and remove pot with other hand. If pot sticks, tap in several places.

4. Gently break roots at bottom of ball and remove any bits of crock or stone. Remove all loose, old compost from top, to a depth of about ½in (1cm). Always handle with care so as not to damage leaves or buds.

6. For large plants in tubs carefully scrape away about 2–3in (5–7cm) old topsoil. Add new compost, leaving ½–¾in (1–1½cm) space between compost and pot rim. Firm down well and water, including feed.

2. Pot offset in new pot, firming compost around base. Water plant well. Keep warm (75°F, (24°C).

Lighting

Houseplants need different amounts of light, but most flowering houseplants prefer a high level of diffused daylight, but not direct sunlight. Diffused light is indirect sunlight, i.e. bouncing off a wall onto the plant or filtering through a net curtain.

Artificial light: To compensate for lack of daylight you can install fluorescent tubes or spotlights. However, conventional artificial light is not as intense as natural daylight and certain plants will not thrive under it.

This problem occurs particularly in offices where either the windows are covered with a solar screen, or where there are no windows at all.

Special horticultural spotlights and fluorescent tubes are available which imitate diffused sunlight more closely and these have a good effect on plants.

Spotlights: To imitate diffused daylight, a blue coating is added to the front of the bulb. The light seems the same as that of a conventional spotlight but in practice plants do actually grow as though they are in daylight. Unfortunately, the problem of heat has not been solved. A 150w reflector lamp mounted closer than 39in (1m) to the plant will overheat its leaves. At 39in (1m) sufficient light will be produced over an area 39in (1m) in diameter but at a distance of 78in (2m), only a quarter of that light will fall on the leaves. Although it is sometimes difficult to position the lights so as to get enough light and not too much heat, spotlights are the most adaptable types.

Fluorescent lights: These are a much more efficient method of providing light and are a popular source of office lighting. They do not give out much heat and are available with a wide range of intensities. Special horticultural tubes fit standard fittings and are available in the same lengths as conventional tubes. They can be combined with standard tubes to give a less stark light. They are obviously not so flexible as spotlights but if a combination of the two types is used, plants in darker areas will benefit. Most specialist plant shops will be able to advise you.

12

Climbers and trailers

Some flowering plants grow very fast. In a greenhouse or permanent sun porch they can be trained around the walls but in ordinary rooms they need a hoop or cane. A simple frame can be made by bending a wire coathanger or using a piece of flexible cane or plastic coated wire.

Training round a hoop

1. Push ends of wire hoop or thin cane so that they are ⅔ down the pot on opposite sides. Bend stem to one side of hoop and gently twist it around the hoop. Do not damage the leaves or stem.

2. Tie a length of twine to one end of hoop and thread it along, looping it loosely around the stem. Do not tie tight knots. The growing tip will continue to follow the line of the hoop. When it reaches the other end, it can be trained round again or twisted back the other way.

Canes

1. A single cane will support a tall plant. Insert cane when repotting, after positioning plant but before adding all the compost. Cane should be a few inches from main stem, stopping about ⅔ down the pot.

A larger support can be made from two canes joined at the top by a stiff wire.

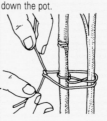

2. Loop a 9in (23cm) length of string around stem and tie in firm knot against cane. Or use a plant ring.

For three plants in one pot, place three canes around pot edge and tie at the top.

Insecticides

Unfortunately some houseplants are vulnerable to pests and diseases. The most common are mealy bug, scale insect, red spider mite and green or whitefly. These should be treated as soon as they are noticed and affected plants moved away from others to prevent the spread of infection. Some pests, such as mealy bug, may also be carried hidden in the soil.

Insecticides are available usually as concentrated liquids which are added to water and sprayed or watered onto the infected plant, and as aerosols ready for use. Systemic insecticides are absorbed into the plant's veins (its system) and so spread the poison to any insect which tries to take nourishment from these.

The least toxic insecticides are those based on pyrethrum and derris as these are both natural substances. They are most suited to whitefly and greenfly control. Derris also controls red spider mite in the early stages. Methylated spirits can be used to remove scale insect and mealy bugs. Red spider can be prevented from recurring by improving humidity. Malathion is one of the most effective general insecticides and will control everything from whitefly to beetles, and especially mealy bug which is one of the most infectious and damaging insects likely to affect houseplants. Other insects such as scale insect and thrips can also be controlled by spraying malathion. It can be sprayed when diluted and also watered into the soil if the soil is infected.

Malathion may damage some sensitive plants, so read the captions carefully to make sure you choose the right treatment for your plant.

Generally insecticides should be applied every 14 days until the pest disappears – but see the instructions for each plant. Fungicides, for mould and fungus infections, generally work with only one application. Check new plants for pests, as they quickly spread from plant to plant. A preventative spray in spring will guard against attack.

Taking care with insecticides

Insecticides and fungicides may contain deadly chemicals. Use them with care.

Never mix different types of insecticides as the chemicals may react.
Never put them into other bottles, such as soft drink or beer bottles.
Never breathe in the spray.
Never spray in windy weather.
Never pour them down the sink or drains. Do not even pour the water in which you have washed containers and sprayers down the drain.
Never make up more at one time than you will use.
Never keep diluted insecticide for more than 24 hours.
Never leave old containers lying around.
Always follow instructions carefully. Do not over or under dilute.

Always use a separate watering can and sprayer, keeping another one for normal spraying and watering.
Always keep away from food, crockery, glasses, food containers, and minerals. Derris is harmful to fish; malathion harms bees.
Always cover fish bowls when spraying.
Always store them with their sprayers and containers in a dry, frost free place, on a high shelf out of reach of children.
Always spray outside, in the evening when bees are not around.
Always wash out all sprayers and empty bottles after use, inside and out.
Always pour washing water onto ground away from food crops and water sources such as streams and rivers.
Always throw empty bottles and containers away with domestic waste.
Always wash thoroughly in hot water and detergent when you have used them.

Flowering maple

The delicate maple-shaped leaves of this plant set off perfectly the slightly waxy looking bell-shaped flowers. The name *Abutilon* is, in fact, the Arabic name for a species of mallow. As a plant in the home, it is rather delicate and needs copious watering in the summer. In the greenhouse, when planted out in the ground, it could reach the rafters; in the house, trained up one or two stakes, it will grow to about 39in (1m). In summer it may be put outside, provided it is sheltered from wind and the temperature is over 60°F (16°C).

The variegated Flowering maple *(Abutilon pictum)* is often grown for the beauty of its leaves alone with flowers as an extra attraction. Green-leaved Flowering maples flower more easily and if kept at 65–70°F (18–21°C) will remain in bloom from summer through to winter.

Light: Diffused (see p.12). If indoors, keep out of midday summer sun. Tolerates full light if put outside in spring, but even outside protect from midday summer sun.

Temperature: 65–70°F (18–21°C) ideal. If kept at this in winter, flowering will continue. Alternatively, keep at 55°F (13°C) and water only once a week.

Water: Almost daily in summer to ensure plant does not dry out, but compost must not be waterlogged. Good drainage essential. In winter when at 55°F (13°C) water only once a week, after surface of compost has dried out.

Humidity: Spray twice weekly in summer, daily if temperature is above 70°F (21°C). Avoid flowers. If plant kept cool, do not spray in winter.

Feeding: Weekly in spring and summer, only after first flowers appear. Use liquid houseplant food diluted to normal strength.

Soil: Equal parts loam-based No. 2, peat and leaf mould, with one-eighth gritty sand.

Repotting: In spring, leaving sufficient space between soil and top of pot to allow for copious summer watering (about 1in, 2½cm).

Cleaning: Spray with soft tepid water. No leafshine. Do not spray flowers.

Webs under leaves. Red spider mite. Remove webs with damp cloth or sponge, then spray with diluted malathion, especially under leaves. Repeat every 14 days until symptoms disappear. Improve humidity by standing pot on saucer of damp pebbles.

Canes

1. Insert cane when repotting, after positioning plant but before adding all the compost. Cane should be a few inches from main stem, stopping about ⅔ down pot. Do not damage roots.

2. Loop string around stem and cane, tying firm knot against cane. Do not tie knot round plant. Or, use a plastic coated 'tie'.

Stem tips flop over. Too hot. Move to a cooler place with more ventilation. Spray daily with soft, tepid water in hot weather.

ant grows pale and raggly with long spaces etween leaves. Too much ht. Move to a shadier position, it of hot summer sun.

ew leaves small, no owers appear. Needs eding. Feed every week in ring and summer after first owers appear. Use liquid use plant food at maker's commended strength.

Plant flops and dies. Too cold. Keep around 55°F (13°C) in winter.

No flowers appear. Too dark and/or needs feeding. Check conditions. Move into lighter place (but not direct sunlight) and feed every week in the growing season with liquid houseplant food diluted to maker's recommended strength.

Flowers turn translucent. Damage from spraying with water. Protect flowers with paper or your hand when spraying leaves.

what goes wrong

Leaves sticky with insects where leaf joins stem. Greenfly. Spray with pyrethrum-based insecticide or diluted malathion. Repeat one week later and then every week until clear.

aves shrivel, flowers fall off summer. Compost too dry. inge pot into bucket of water 10–15 minutes, then drain. ep soil constantly moist in mmer, watering every day if dries out in hot weather. not allow to stand in water. ray daily with soft tepid ter if temperature above °F (21°C).

Flies hopping around compost surface. Whitefly. Spray with pyrethrum-based insecticide or diluted malathion. Repeat weekly until clear.

Leaves fall off in winter. Compost too wet. Keep almost dry from end of autumn to spring in a temperature of 55°F (13°C). Water only when compost surface feels dry, about once a week.

15

Lipstick vine

The Lipstick vine is similar in general appearance to a *Columnea* (p.44). The main difference is in the flowers, which have four stamens and are more tubular in shape. The plant is best grown in a hanging pot or basket. The dark crimson flowers have an orange throat which contrasts with the dark green fleshy foliage. Pinch out flower buds during its first year, but encourage growth of stems and leaves by frequent watering. The following winter it should be kept cool and dry to rest it. Next year it will bloom profusely.

The Lipstick vine looks at its best in a hanging container and can be planted into a moss-lined basket when it it is 2 years old. For its first three years it should be kept out of direct sunlight, in a constantly humid atmosphere.

Light: Indirect daylight (see p.12) when plant is young. It will take full light after 3 years, avoiding midday sun.
Temperature: 75-80°F (24-27°C) in summer; winter minimum is 60°F (16°C).
Water: Every 2 days in spring and summer, especially in first year. When over 75°C, (24°C) never let compost dry out. Check it daily. Water in winter only about once a week, when compost surface feels dry.
Humidity: Spray daily all spring and summer, as very high humidity essential for good growth. In winter, spray weekly only if temperature is above 60°F (16°C).
Feeding: Once every 14 days in spring and summer after first flowers appear, using liquid houseplant food diluted to maker's instructions (see p.8).
Soil: Equal parts rough sand and rich fibrous peat with one-eighth part chopped sphagnum moss added. Put charcoal and broken crocks in bottom of pot or basket.
Repotting: Annually in early years. Alternatively, plant in basket lined with sphagnum moss; or grow plant on a wooden block covered with green moss. The roots should be wrapped in sphagnum moss and fixed to the block with copper wire.
Cleaning: No leafshine.

Hanging baskets

1. Line wire basket with moss. Make 5 or 6 small holes in sheet of polythene and lay over moss. Add saucer of charcoal to absorb smells.

2. Stand basket on bucket and fill with layer of damp compost.

3. Knock plant from pot and place in centre of basket, arranging trailing stems evenly all round.

4. Fill with compost and firm round roots. Water well, allow to drain, then hang securely. Fasten drip tray below.

o flowers in second year, new leaves
mall. Pot too large and needs feeding. It
owers better if slightly pot bound, so do
ot repot again for 2 years. Feed every 2
eeks in spring and summer when flowers
ppear, with liquid houseplant food diluted
 maker's recommended strength.

ebs under leaves. Red
ider mite. Remove webs
ith damp cloth or sponge,
en spray with diluted
alathion, especially under
aves. Repeat every 14 days
til symptoms disappear.
prove humidity by standing
ot on saucer of wet pebbles.

ant wilts in summer. Too
ot and compost too dry.
unge pot into bucket of
ater for 10–15 minutes
en drain. Keep compost
nstantly moist in summer,
atering every day if it dries
t in hot weather.

eaves drop. In winter, too
ld. Move to warmer place,
 least 60°F (16°C). In
mmer if leaves drop and
 flowers appear, too cold
d dry. Move to warmer
ace, but not more than
°F (27°C) and water by
nging pot into bucket of
ater for 10–15 minutes.

*Flowers turn black and fall
in summer.* Air too dry.
Spray daily with soft, tepid
water and stand pot on saucer
of wet pebbles.

*Leaves dry out, especially
in summer.* Air too dry. Spray
daily in spring and summer
with soft tepid water and
provide extra humidity by
standing pot on saucer of
wet pebbles.

*Black spots on leaves,
especially in winter.* Botrytis,
plant too cold and wet. Spray
with fungicide then place in
warmer atmosphere, at least
60°F (16°C). Allow surface of
compost to dry out between
waterings in winter and spray
less often. Remove affected
leaves.

*Plant stems grow long and
straggly.* Too dark. Move to
position in very good light
including some direct sun.

17

Golden trumpet

This is an evergreen flowering plant originating in tropical America. It will climb to its maximum height of 10ft (3m) in 4 years. After flowering, it should be cut back to one joint of the old wood in midwinter, when it should be allowed to rest. It is an easily grown plant, preferring a warm greenhouse or conservatory, though it will grow well in the home if humidity is high. It should not be kept near radiators nor should it ever become waterlogged as the roots will stagnate and begin to rot.

The Golden trumpet is an evergreen climber with attractive trumpet-shaped yellow flowers. Plants are usually bought when 12–18in (30–45cm) high but will easily grow to 10ft (3m) tall, when they will need the support of canes or a trellis.

Light: Full in summer, slight shade in winter when temperature below 60°F (16°C).
Temperature: Maintain 70–80°F (21–27°C) in summer, less in winter, with minimum of 55°F (13°C).
Water: Copiously when growing to keep always moist, i.e. almost daily if temperatures high. From late summer to early spring, water only when compost surface feels quite dry, once a week or less.
Humidity: Spray every 2 days in spring and summer to maintain moist atmosphere, avoiding flowers. Place pot on saucer of pebbles almost covered with water.
Feeding: Weekly in spring and summer after first flowers appear, using liquid houseplant food diluted to maker's instructions (see p.8).
Soil: Two parts loam-based No. 2 to 1 part peat and charcoal or coarse sand with one-eighth part rotten cow manure if available.
Repotting: For new plants, as soon as roots grow through bottom of pot, i.e. every month for 3 months, using pot next size up and firming compost around old root ball. After first year, repot annually as soon as new growth starts and certainly not after it has grown 6in (15cm).
Cleaning: Spray with tepid soft water, avoiding flowers. No leafshine.

Webs under leaves. Red spider mite. Remove webs with damp cloth or sponge, then spray with diluted malathion, especially under leaves. Repeat every 14 days until symptoms disappear. Improve humidity by standing pot on saucer of wet pebbles.

Plant goes limp. In summer, compost too dry. In winter, too cold and wet. If dry, plunge pot into bucket of water for 10–15 minutes, then drain. Keep compost constantly moist in summer, watering every day if it dries out. In winter, water only when compost surface feels quite dry. Minimum winter temperature 55°F (13°C).

No flowers appear. Too dark and/or needs feeding. Check conditions. Move into lighter place (but not in direct sunlight) and feed weekly when flowering with liquid houseplant food diluted according to instructions.

New leaves small. Needs feeding. Feed with liquid houseplant food every week when flowering, diluting food to recommended strength.

Whole plant turns black. Leafshine damage. Do not use. Clean only by carefully dusting with feather duster or camel hair brush.

Pruning

1. To keep them compact and to make sure of continued flowering, plants over 2 or 3 years old should be pruned in early spring.

2. Cut stems back to about 6in (16cm) above compost, just above a leaf.

Plant grows very leggy. Not enough light and needs pruning. Move into light position (but not in direct sunlight). Prune in spring.

what goes wrong

Leaves curl up in winter. Too cold. Move to warmer place above 55°F (13°C).

Leaves curl and turn brown in summer. Too cold. Move to warmer place. Do not allow temperature in summer to fall below 70°F (21°C). Try to keep at 70–80°F (21–27°C).

Leaves turn black, stems rot. Too cold and damp, especially in winter. Spray with fungicide then place in warmer atmosphere and spray and water less often.

White cotton-wool patches where leaf joins stem. Mealy bug. Spray with diluted malathion and remove bugs and 'wool' with tweezers. Repeat every 14 days until symptoms disappear. Or, paint bugs with methylated spirits and remove with tweezers.

19

Anthurium andreanum

Wax flower

The flowers of this plant are much used by flower arrangers, especially in Japanese floristry and to produce highly stylised displays. They are often mistaken for artificial ones as they have an unreal, waxy appearance. Whether cut or growing, the flowers can last several weeks. Warmth, moisture and humidity are all important for this plant.

If kept in high humidity, Wax flowers will produce a succession of their exotic, waxy blooms from spring to late summer. Flowers are usually red but white and pink varieties are occasionally available.

Light: Full diffused light (see p.12) but not direct sunlight.
Temperature: 70°F (21°C) all year is ideal. Tolerates maximum 85°F (29°C) for short periods provided humidity is high. Winter minimum 60°F (16°C). Try to keep around 60°F (16°C) for 6 weeks in late winter, before flowers appear.
Water: Copiously with soft water at least twice weekly in spring and summer to keep compost always moist. In winter, enough to keep roots just moist at all times, about once a week.
Humidity: Spray daily in spring and summer, once or twice a week in winter. In hot weather stand pot on saucer of pebbles almost covered with water. Keep moss around roots moist.
Feeding: Every 14 days in summer with liquid houseplant food diluted to maker's instructions (see p.8).
Soil: Equal parts chopped sphagnum moss and peat-based compost. Good drainage essential.
Repotting: In winter, with above compost mixture and plenty of crocks in bottom of pot. Spread roots carefully, pack compost round them. Plant base should stand 2-3in (5-7cm) above pot level with moss around exposed roots.
Cleaning: Wipe leaves with damp cloth. Use leafshine every 8 weeks.

Webs on leaves. Red spider mite. Remove webs with damp cloth or sponge, then spray with diluted malathion, especially under leaves. Repeat every 14 days until symptoms disappear. Improve humidity by standing pot on saucer of wet pebbles.

Leaves split and become diseased. Split caused by physical damage but leaf may then rot. Cut off damaged leaf at base of stem.

Discs on leaves. Scale insect. Spray underside of leaves with diluted malathion and, after 48 hours, remove discs with thumbnail. Repeat every week for 4 weeks until clear.

what goes wrong

Leaves lose gloss. Air too dry. Spray daily in spring and summer with soft tepid water, once or twice a week in winter.

No flowers appear. Too dark. Move to position in good light but not direct sunlight. Or, overwatered previous winter. Water only once a week in winter.

Lush foliage but no flowers. Compost too rich. Repot in winter using correct mixture (see p.20) not loam-based.

New leaves small and pale, no flowers appear. Needs feeding. Feed every 14 days in summer with liquid houseplant food diluted to recommended strength.

Leaves yellow and curl under in winter. Too cold and wet. Move to warmer place, above 60°F (16°C) and allow compost surface to dry out before watering again. Try to keep temperature even. If leaves curl while green, cold draughts. Move plant to protected position.

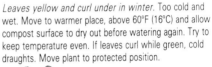

Leaves look dry and papery, with yellowish colour. Too dry. Water immediately and keep compost always moist.

Leaves turn black. Too cold, possibly by cold glass in winter. Keep around 70°F (21°C) in summer and at least 60°F (16°C) in winter.

Brown spots on leaves. Fungus. Spray with systemic fungicide. If leaf badly affected, remove.

White cotton-wool patches under leaves and at leaf base. Mealy bug. Spray with diluted malathion and remove bugs and 'wool' with tweezers. Repeat every 14 days until clear. Or, paint bugs with methylated spirits and remove with tweezers.

Flies hopping around plant. Whitefly. Spray with pyrethrum-based insecticide or diluted malathion. Repeat one week later, then every week until clear.

Roots push up more than 3in (7cm) above soil, raising plant on stilts. Needs repotting but do not do so unless it is winter. Pack moss between and around roots.

Zebra plant

Bright yellow pagoda-shaped flowers form on the tips of the leaf stems of this native of tropical and sub-tropical America. The striped foliage looks strong but *Aphelandras* can be tricky to keep. They should never dry out in the growing season; once they have flowered they should have a 6-week rest period, with water cut down to once a week.

Light: Full diffused daylight all round plant; no direct sunlight, or plant wilts.

Temperature: Daytime maximum 80°F (27°C), night temperature 65°F (18°C) in summer. When plant resting after flowering, reduce day temperature to 65°F (18°C) and night temperature to 50–55°C (10–13°F). In winter daytime minimum 60°F (16°C).

Zebra plants are commonly available but fairly difficult to keep, the lush, striped foliage being liable to flop unless well watered when growing. A dormant period after the spring and summer flowering is the secret of keeping plant from year to year.

Water: At least twice a week in spring and summer to keep moist. Once flowering has stopped, water only when compost surface feels dry, but plant must not shrivel. Once a week should be sufficient.

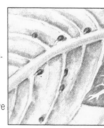

Leaves have mottled patches around small, disc-like marks. Scale insect. Paint discs on underside of leaves with methylated spirits. After 48 hours remove discs with thumbnail.

Humidity: Spray daily with soft water in growing season. Stand pot on saucer of pebbles almost covered with water. Reduce humidity when plant is resting or in low temperatures (below 55°F, 13°C).

Feeding: Every 14 days after first flower buds appear, using liquid houseplant food diluted to maker's instructions (see p.8). Do not feed in winter.

Soil: Equal parts loam-based No.2 and peat with one-eighth part sand added.

Repotting: In early spring after dormant period for plants more than 2 years old. Remove as much old compost as possible and use 5in (13cm) maximum pot size. Larger pots encourage straggly plants.

Cleaning: Spray with tepid water, avoiding flowers. If leaves dusty, wipe with damp cloth. No leafshine.

Humidity

Spray every day in summer, once a week in winter. Protect flowers. For extra humidity, stand the pot on a saucer of pebbles. Add water to almost cover the pebbles but do not let the base of the pot touch the water or the roots will become waterlogged.

what goes wrong

Flies hopping around flower. Blackfly or greenfly. Spray every 14 days until clear with pyrethrum-based insecticide.

New leaves stay small. Needs feeding. Add liquid houseplant food to the water every 14 days after flower buds appear. Dilute food to maker's recommended strength.

White cotton-wool patches where leaf joins stem. Mealy bug. Spray every week until clear with diluted malathion and remove bugs and 'wool' with tweezers.

Base of stem rots. Too cold and wet. Move to warmer place and maintain at least 60°F (16°C). Allow compost to dry out before watering again. Then keep moist but do not allow to stand in water.

Leaves fall. Too dry or in a draught. Water first by plunging pot in bucket of water for 10 minutes. Drain and place in draught-free place. Then water twice weekly in spring and summer, weekly in winter.

Plant grows very tall and straggly. Needs pruning, or kept too warm in winter. Keep cool (about 55°F, 13°C) for 6 weeks after flowering, allowing soil to dry out between waterings. Prune in spring.

Plant does not flower. Pot too large. Repot in early spring into smaller pot, trimming away excess roots. Prune following spring, then start feeding as soon as flower buds appear.

Flower droops and leaves look limp. Plant beginning to dry out, too wet and/or too hot. Check conditions. If dry, water well and plant should recover. Keep compost moist while growing and flowering, but never leave pot standing in water: a waterlogged plant may show same symptoms. Check temperature (see p.22) and keep out of direct sunlight.

Leaves turn pale. Too dark. Move into light position, but not in direct sunlight.

Brown spots on leaves. Too much sun. Move out of direct sunlight, into position of good diffused daylight.

Brown patches on leaves. Caused by smoke or gas fire fumes. Keep in clean atmosphere and cut off marked leaves as close to main stem as possible.

Webs under leaves, leaves eventually discolour and fall. Red spider mite. Spray every week with diluted malathion for four weeks. Improve humidity around plant by standing pot on saucer of wet pebbles.

23

Azalea

This spectacular winter-flowering house-plant is a member of the Rhododendron family. Unlike other azaleas, *Azalea indica* is not hardy and will not survive frost if planted in the garden after flowering. Its most important requirement is copious amounts of soft water, both watered on and sprayed. It grows very slowly and would naturally flower in spring, but is usually 'forced' to produce flowers from early winter.

Azaleas are winter-flowering indoor plants which do best in a cool atmosphere and give great pleasure at a time when few plants are in flower. Plants are available to 18in (45cm) in height and diameter, although more expensive standards and pyramids can also be obtained.

Light: Plenty of diffused light (see p.12) but keep out of direct sun.

Temperature: Maintain 55°F (13°C) all winter, though up to 60–65°F (16–18°C) can be tolerated for short periods if humidity is high. Once in bud, keep under 55°F (13°C).

Water: Copiously. Best method is to plunge pot into bucket of soft, lime-free water so that compost surface is covered. Leave until bubbles stop rising (about 10 minutes) then drain for half an hour before replacing in usual position. Do not leave for long periods standing in water. Do not allow compost to dry out: water every day all year round if necessary to keep it moist.

Humidity: Spray daily all year round with soft water, avoiding flowers. Stand pot on saucer of wet pebbles.

Feeding: Start feeding when flower buds form in early autumn, then feed weekly until spring. Reduce to fortnightly and stop feeding at midsummer. Use liquid house-plant food diluted to maker's instructions.

Soil: Equal parts of leafmould, peat and pine needles, with ¼ part sharp sand added.

Repotting: In summer, sink pot in ground outside in shady place. Keep watered and sprayed. In early autumn repot in 1 size larger pot. Clay pots are best.

Cleaning: Humidity spraying adequate. No leafshine.

Flowers have black marks. Leafshine or insecticide damage. Do not use leafshine at all and do not spray flowers with insecticides of any kind.

Leaves have black marks. Leafshine damage. Do not use.

Leaves and flowers dry up and fall. Insufficient watering, too hot and air too dry or too wet. Check conditions. If dry, plunge pot into bucket of water and leave until bubbles stop rising. Allow to drain before replacing in position. Repeat daily in hot weather and spray daily all year round with tepid soft water. Keep in cooler place, around 55°F (13°C) ideal. If compost completely waterlogged, plant may show same symptoms: drain water from saucer and allow compost surface to dry out before watering again.

Leaves become hairy. Natural, do not remove them.

Plant grows straggly and out of shape. Needs pruning. Prune after flowering, removing lanky stems that grow from flower clusters.

New leaves stay small, flowers do not form. Needs feeding. Feed once a week from time first buds appear and while flowering with liquid houseplant food diluted in water or with a foliar feed when spraying. After flowering feed fortnightly. Stop feeding in midsummer.

Watering

Water by plunging pot into large bowl or bucket so that water covers pot rim. Spray leaves. Leave for 15 minutes, then take pot out and allow it to drain. Always use soft water.

what goes wrong

Flowers fail to open. Waterlogged, standing in water or too hot. Check conditions. Always drain away excess water 10–15 minutes after watering. Spray daily with tepid soft water and keep at around 55°F (13°C). If waterlogged, allow compost surface to dry out.

Leaves turn pale green. Too dark or lime damage, eventually killing plant. If in dark place, move to lighter position; will take full sun. Check compost is lime-free and water and spray only with soft water.

White rings on leaves. Azalea leaf miner. Spray leaves with diluted malathion. Repeat once after 1 week. Do not spray flowers.

Brown husks around flowers. Natural. They will fall as flower develops.

Leaves turn black. Too cold. Move to warmer place, over 50°F (10°C).

Leaves have yellow speckles and webs underneath. Red spider

Flies hopping around plant. Whitefly. Spray with pyrethrum-based insecticide, avoiding flowers if possible. Repeat every 14 days until clear.

mite. Spray with diluted malathion, avoiding flowers which will burn. Repeat weekly for 4 weeks. Continue daily spraying with tepid soft water.

Begonia

Begonias are divided into three main categories, tuberous, rhizomatous, and fibrous-rooted. Tuberous begonias are descended from species introduced in 1865; even today hybrid varieties show traces of the foliage markings of *Begonia pearcei* from which they originated. The tubers are planted in early spring and by late spring have developed into young plants which will flower in summer.

The tuberous Begonia flowers from summer to early autumn. Many colours are available including red, orange, yellow, and shades of pink. They are usually sold as plants from early summer to the end of autumn but the tubers can be stored over winter and replanted in spring.

Light: Full diffused light (see p.12), but not direct sun.

Temperature: Summer maximum 70°F (21°C), minimum 60°F (16°C). In winter, store tubers in dry place at 50–55°F (10–13°C).

Water: Start watering dormant and divided tubers in early spring, watering whenever surface becomes dry; in summer, copiously once a week as surface begins to dry. If temperature drops below 60°F (16°C), water only when surface is dry, or tuber will rot.

Humidity: Spray weekly if temperature above 70°F (21°C). Stand pot on saucer of pebbles almost covered with water.

Feeding: Monthly after flower buds formed, with liquid food diluted to maker's instructions (see p.8).

Soil: Plant new or divided tubers in equal parts peat and sand. When repotting shoots, use loam-based No.2.

Repotting: Plant or repot tubers in early spring in 3–4in (7–10cm) pots. When shoots are 3–4in (7–10cm) long, repot into 4–5in (10–14cm) pots. In winter, when leaves have died down and compost quite dry, remove tubers and store between layers of newspaper in cool, dry place. Alternatively, tubers can be left dry in their pots.

Cleaning: Not necessary, though may be dusted gently with soft brush. No leafshine.

Leaves have black patches. Botrytis. Too cold and damp. Spray with fungicide, then place in warmer atmosphere and spray with water less often. Allow compost surface to dry out between temperature 60°F (16°C). Remove damaged leaves.

Yellow patches on leaves. Begonia mite. Remove affected leaves and burn them. Dust plant with sulphur immediately, then once a month for 3 months.

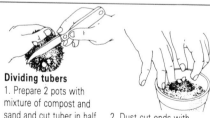

Dividing tubers
1. Prepare 2 pots with mixture of compost and sand and cut tuber in half with sharp knife. Each section must include a shoot and roots.

2. Dust cut ends with sulphur dust and pot each separately, with half tuber above compost.

what goes wrong

Leaves turn yellow. Too cold and wet. Move to warmer place, at least 60°F (16°C) and allow surface of soil to dry out before watering again. Water only when surface of soil dries out, once a week in summer should be enough.

Flowers turn transparent. Damage from water spray. When spraying plant, protect flowers by shielding with paper or your hand. Remove damaged flower.

Brown spots on flowers. Damage from water spray. Protect flowers with paper or your hand when spraying leaves. Remove damaged lower at base of its stem.

Leaves small and no flowers appear. Needs feeding. Feed once a month after flower buds form with houseplant food diluted to maker's recommended strength. If leaves grow sparsely, too dark. Plant needs good diffused light to grow well and produce flowers.

Brown scorch marks on leaves and flowers. Damage by sunlight. Move into an area of diffused daylight, out of direct sun. Remove damaged leaves and flowers.

Leaves droop and dry up. Too hot. Move to cooler place with more ventilation. Spray daily with soft, tepid water, avoiding flowers. Maximum temperature 70°F (21°C).

Stems go squashy. Too cold and damp or plant waterlogged, standing in water. Check conditions and move to position at least 60°F (16°C). Allow compost surface to dry out before watering again and drain away any water from saucer below plant. If there are signs of mould, spray stems with fungicide.

Tips of leaves curl, plant flops. Too dry. Keep soil moist in summer, watering copiously once a week, just as surface begins to feel dry.

27

Beloperone guttata

Shrimp plant

This plant takes its name from its shrimp-like pink bract, its flowers being white and comparatively insignificant. Since Shrimp plants come from tropical America, they are ideally suited to a heated greenhouse in the growing season and in the home need care, especially if in a centrally heated house which may be hot and dry at some times but cold if unoccupied during the day. If the temperature drops, watch that the atmosphere is not too humid or the bracts may rot: this is not a suitable plant for a bathroom, for example. In winter, when the plant is not growing, it should be kept cooler and drier than in the growing season and may lose some of its leaves.

The pink shrimp-like bracts of the Shrimp plant are its main attraction; the true flowers are small and white. Bracts and flowers appear in summer when the plant is usually available at a height of about 10–12in (25–30cm).

Light: Full light, including direct sunlight in summer. Keep in shady place in winter.

Temperature: 65°F (18°C) in spring and summer. 45°F (7°C) in winter, when plant tends to lose leaves.

Water: Profusely in summer to keep always moist, though good drainage essential. Water every day in hot weather if necessary. Water in winter only when compost surface seems dry, about once a week.

Humidity: Stand pot on saucer of pebbles almost covered with water to maintain reasonable humidity. Do not spray bracts.

Feeding: Every 3 weeks after flowering begins to end of summer, using liquid houseplant food diluted to half maker's recommended strength (see p.8).

Soil: Loam-based No. 2 with good drainage.

Repotting: Prune straggly plants in early spring and repot into next size pot until in 5in (13cm). When in this size, simply remove plant from pot, knock off old compost and replace with new in same container.

Cleaning: Not necessary. If dusty spray leaves only with soft, tepid water. No leafshine. Remove dead bracts immediately.

Pruning

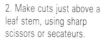

1. In spring, prune straggly plants before repotting and before buds appear.

2. Make cuts just above a leaf stem, using sharp scissors or secateurs.

3. Dead or discoloured bracts should be removed as they occur. Pinch them off with thumb and forefinger above first pair of leaves.

what goes wrong

Plant straggly and tall. Too hot and needs pruning. Move to cooler place, (65°F, 18°C) in spring and summer, 45°F (7°C) in winter. Prune in spring.

Bracts turn black. Spraying damage. When flower bracts appear, do not spray. Create humidity by standing pot on saucer of damp pebbles. Remove damaged bract at its base.

Bracts stay pale. Too dark in summer or too hot in winter. In summer, move to lighter position: plant will take full sun. Keep shaded in winter. If kept cool in winter (45°F, 7°C), bracts will have stronger colour.

Leaves turn black after cleaning. Leafshine damage. Do not use. Clean by spraying with soft, tepid water.

Leaves distorted and sticky, with small insects. Greenfly. Spray every week for 4 weeks with pyrethrum-based insecticide.

Leaves yellow with webs underneath. Red spider mite. Spray leaves with diluted malathion every 14 days until clear. Do not spray bracts or they will burn. Improve humidity.

Leaves pale. Needs feeding. Feed every 3 weeks from first buds to end of summer with houseplant food diluted to half maker's recommended strength.

Leaves turn yellow. Too wet, waterlogged. Check drainage in pot and allow compost to dry out before watering again. Never leave standing in water.

Leaves drop in summer. Too dry. Water compost. Keep moist throughout summer but do not allow to become waterlogged. In winter, too cold. Move to warmer place; 45°F (7°C) ideal temperature. Keep compost barely moist, allowing top layer to dry out between waterings.

Flowers drop. Natural; flowers fall about 1 week after emerging from bract but bracts remain healthy for much longer.

Billbergia nutans

Queen's tears

This evergreen flowering plant belongs to the large plant family known as Bromeliads. Individual plants have a limited life-span (2–3 years) and usually flower only once. However, the flowers and coloured bracts last for a long time and when the parent plant dies, it produces offsets at its base which can be carefully removed and potted up as new plants. It is almost hardy and will tolerate very low, though not freezing temperatures.

Light: Tolerates full sunlight for short periods, but prefers high levels of diffused light (see p.12).
Temperature: 65–80°F (18–27°C) in summer. 60–70°F (16–21°C) in winter, though will tolerate 45°F (7°C) at night if kept dry.
Water: Twice a week with soft water in summer, allowing some water to fill central rosette of stems. In winter, if temperature is low (45°F, 7°C), water only every 14 days to keep compost dry and do not fill central well; otherwise, water weekly.
Humidity: Spraying usually unnecessary. Plant is very tolerant, though does not like very humid atmosphere if temperature below 50°F (10°C), or very dry atmosphere when in flower.
Feeding: Not necessary, provided plant is repotted annually.
Soil: Equal parts loam-based No. 2, rough peat and leafmould or silver sand.
Repotting: Annually in late spring. When offsets appear, the parent plant will eventually die. When offsets are at least 5in (13cm) long, they can be carefully separated and potted up. They will develop quickly into mature plants, but will not flower for 2 years.
Cleaning: Spray dusty plants with soft, tepid water, avoiding flowers. No leafshine.

The Queen's tears plant is a bromeliad with fairly plain, long, pointed leaves and fascinating rose-coloured bracts out of which grow clusters of long pendulous flowers. It can survive very low temperatures so is ideal for homes where the heating is off during the day.

Removing offsets

1. When flowers and leaves of parent plant have quite died down, offset will be about half the size of parent and will be ready to separate. Prepare small pot with drainage layer and mixture of damp peat and sand.

2. Knock plant from pot and cut offset and its roots from old plant with a sharp knife.

3. Place offset in new pot and firm compost around its base, covering roots. Water well and cover pot with polythene for 2–3 days to provide extra humidity. Discard parent plant.

Plant does not flower. Not enough light and/or pot too large. Move to position in good light: it will stand direct sunshine. They flower better if slightly pot bound but will only flower once in their 3-year life cycle.

what goes wrong

Leaves dry out and turn brown. Compost too dry. Plunge pot into bucket of water for 10–15 minutes, then drain. Keep compost constantly moist in summer, watering twice a week or as soon as surface begins to dry out; make sure drainage is good as must not become waterlogged. Keep water in central well.

Leaves turn black. Leafshine damage. Do not use. Clean only by spraying with soft, tepid water. Remove damaged leaf. If many are affected, plant will not recover.

Flowers dry out. Air too dry. Provide extra humidity by standing pot on saucer of wet pebbles.

Leaves curl. In summer, too cold. Move to warmer place and do not allow temperature to fall below 65°F (18°C). In winter, too hot or too wet. Best between 60-70°F (16-21°C) in winter. If in colder place (45°F, 7°C) do not water compost or well.

Leaves turn soft and mushy with grey mouldy patches. Botrytis. Plant much too wet and cold. Allow surface of compost to dry out before watering again and keep above 65°F (18°) in summer. If 45°F (7°C) in winter, keep much drier, with no water in central well.

Stamens of flowers rot. Too wet, overwatered or standing in water. Allow surface of compost to dry out between waterings. In winter if in cool place (45°F, 7°C), water only once every 14 days with no water in well.

White cotton-wool patches round base of plant. Mealy bug. Spray with diluted malathion and remove bugs and 'wool' with tweezers. Repeat every 14 days until symptoms disappear. Or, paint bugs with methylated spirits and remove with tweezers.

Flies hopping around plant. Whitefly. Spray with pyrethrum-based insecticide or diluted malathion. Repeat every week until clear.

Trompetilla

Named after a 17th-century horticulturalist, Dr Charles Bouvard, this plant originated in Mexico. It was once used for its medicinal properties against dysentry and hydrophobia (rabies). In Victorian times it was a popular indoor flowering plant, especially in the conservatory, and its flowers were used for buttonholes and table decorations. Some of its varieties, such as *Bouvardia humboldtii* and *jasminiflora,* are strongly scented.

Light: Full but diffused daylight (see p.12). Keep out of direct sunlight.
Temperature: Summer minimum 65°F (18°C), and maximum 85°F (29°C), but ventilation must be good. Winter minimum 55°F (13°C), keeping plant away from radiators.
Water: At least twice weekly from late spring to summer, so that compost is always moist. Reduce to once a week or less in winter, allowing surface to dry between waterings. Do not stand plant in water.
Humidity: Spray weekly in spring and summer, avoiding flowers and stopping if temperature falls below 65°F (18°C). Stand pot on saucer of pebbles almost covered with water. In winter do not spray plant, and remove from saucer of pebbles.
Feeding: Every 14 days in summer, with liquid houseplant food diluted to half maker's recommended strength (see p.8). Do not feed during rest of year.
Soil: Equal parts of peat, loam-based No.3, leafmould, peat and silver sand.
Repotting: In late spring into pot 5in (13cm) maximum size. In early spring, before repotting, prune to shorten previous year's growth. Cut to 1in (2.5cm) above base of plant, cutting just above a leaf.
Cleaning: Humidity spraying adequate. No leafshine.

The Trompetilla's clusters of flowers appear from summer to late autumn and were once popular as buttonholes and table decorations. Its growing tips must be pinched out regularly to keep it bushy and compact.

Insects crawling around flower buds. Greenfly. Spray with pyrethrum-based insecticide or diluted malathion. Repeat one week later, then every week until clear.

what goes wrong

White cotton-wool patches where leaf joins stem. Mealy bug. Spray with diluted malathion and remove bugs and 'wool' with tweezers. Repeat every 14 days until symptoms disappear. Or, paint bugs with methylated spirits and remove with tweezers.

Pruning

Unless growing tips are pinched out, plant will grow straggly and not flower well. With tips of fingers, pinch out small pair of leaves at end of stems every 2 weeks. Treat one-third of stems each time.

Whole plant flops. In summer, compost too dry or too cold. Check conditions. If temperature below 65°F (18°C) move to warmer position. If soil dry, plunge pot into bucket of water for 10–15 minutes, then drain. If plant flops in winter, too wet, overwatered. Water only when compost surface has dried out.

No flowers appear. Too dark. Move into light position but not in direct sunlight.

Black marks on leaves. Too cold or leafshine damage. Move to warmer place, at least 65°F (18°C) in summer, 55°F (13°C) in winter and never use leafshine.

Webs under leaves. Red spider mite. Remove webs with damp cloth or sponge, then spray with diluted malathion, especially under leaves. Repeat every 14 days until symptoms disappear. Improve humidity.

New leaves small. Needs feeding. Feed every week while growing and flowering with houseplant food at half recommended strength.

Leaves are soft and mushy. Too cold and damp, humidity too high. Spray with fungicide then place in warmer atmosphere, at least 55°F (13°C) in winter. Spray with water less often and allow soil to dry out between waterings in winter.

Leaves dry out. Too hot and too sunny. Move to cooler place with more ventilation and out of direct sunlight. Keep under 85°F (29°C) if possible.

Plant grows straggly and out of shape with no flowers. Pinch out some growing tips every 2 weeks throughout growing season until late summer when plant should be bushy and about 18in (50cm) in diameter.

Brunfelsia calycina

Yesterday-today-and-tomorrow

When this plant's first flush of flowers has died, a second flowering can sometimes be brought about by lowering the temperature (see below). Plants over two years old flower more profusely than young ones. Propagation is easiest by cuttings. Root them in sand and put in a warm place under a glass bell or clear polythene bag. Pot them up in the usual compost with ¼ part sand added.

Light: Keep shaded from direct sunlight when growing and in flower. Put in direct sunlight after flowering.

Temperature: Maintain 60–70°F (16–21°C) in spring and summer. After first flowering, reduce temperature to 55°F (13°C). This will encourage a second flush of flowers. After second flowering, reduce temperature to about 48°F (9°C) to harden plant, when green shoots will turn woody.

Water: Twice weekly in spring and summer to keep moist. Once every 2 weeks in autumn and winter to allow compost to dry out.

Humidity: Needs high humidity in spring and summer but do not spray once flowers appear. Stand pot on saucer of pebbles almost covered with water, or plant into another container of damp peat to maintain high humidity. In winter, reduce humidity to keep drier.

Feeding: Once in spring with nitrogen-based fertilizer to stop leaves becoming pale. Feed monthly when growing with liquid houseplant food diluted to half maker's recommended strength (see p.8).

Soil: Equal parts loam-based No. 2 and peat.

Repotting: In autumn as soon as flowering is over, into pots one size larger. Prune lightly following spring.

Cleaning: Spray with soft tepid water only when not in flower, and not in winter. No leafshine.

The plant known as Yesterday-today-tomorrow flowers in late spring and summer, producing an abundance of delicate, scented purple flowers which slowly change colour through to white before they are finished. To keep the plant compact, prune it lightly after the flowers have finished.

Plant grows straggly in spring. Needs pruning. Prune in spring, cutting back stems above a leaf to within 6in (15cm) of pot.

Preparing a cutting

1. Cut off tip of healthy stem including 2 pairs of leaves and growing point. Trim off stem below a leaf.

2. Remove lowest pair of leaves so there is a section of bare stem. When planted, lowest leaf should be just above compost.

3. Keep moist and warm (65–70°F, 18–21°C) for 21 days. Cover with polythene bag to keep humid, removing it for 5 minutes a day.

Foliage grows fast but no flowers appear. Too much feeding. Feed once a month only with liquid houseplant food diluted to half maker's recommended strength.

Webs under leaves. Red spider mite. Remove webs with damp cloth or sponge, then spray with diluted malathion, especially under leaves. Repeat every 14 days until symptoms disappear. Improve humidity by standing on saucer of wet pebbles.

Plant flops in summer. Too wet, waterlogged. Drain away any water from saucer and allow compost surface to dry out before watering again. Check drainage in pot.

Grey mould on leaves and stems, no growth. Too wet in winter. Keep above 40°F (7°C) and allow compost to dry out between waterings.

Leaves pale and limp. In summer, too much light. Move to shaded place, out of direct sunlight. In winter, not enough light. Move to position in very good light – will stand full sun in winter but not in summer.

Leaves pale in spring. Lack of nitrogen. Feed once only with nitrogen-based fertilizer, then monthly with half-strength houseplant food.

Leaves turn black. Leafshine damage. Do not use. Remove damaged leaf.

Flowers turn brown and fall off quickly, leaves fall later. Compost too dry. Plunge pot into bucket of water for 10–15 minutes, then drain. Keep compost constantly moist in summer, watering twice weekly or every day if it dries out in very hot weather. Do not stand in water. Spray daily with soft tepid water, avoiding flowers. If flowers are scorched, too much direct sun. Move into more shady place.

Leaves dry out in summer. Too hot and air too dry. Move to cooler place with more ventilation and stand pot on saucer of wet pebbles to improve humidity. Do not keep above 60–70°F (16–21°C) in summer if possible.

Leaves turn brown and fall off in winter. Too hot. Move to cooler place with more ventilation and spray daily with soft, tepid water. Maximum winter temperature 48°F (9°C).

what goes wrong

Camellia japonica

Tea plant

These small evergreen shrubs produce strikingly uniform flowers in various strong colours, set against lush dark green leaves. They require good light to ensure flower buds form plentifully but dislike a hot, dry centrally heated atmosphere. In a cooler room, porch or conservatory where they can be kept at the right temperature and humidity, they will flourish.

Light: Full light, but plant should be kept out of bright midday sun.
Temperature: 65-70°F (18-21°C) in spring and summer to keep plant warm when growing. 55°F (13°C) in autumn and winter until flowers open, when temperature should be increased to 60°F (16°C).
Water: Twice weekly in spring to keep compost moist but plant must not stand in water. Weekly or less in summer only when compost surface dries out. Increase to twice weekly from autumn on, with good drainage in pot. Always use softened lime-free or rainwater.
Humidity: Spray weekly with soft tepid water all year except when in flower.
Feeding: Once in early spring with sequestered iron, then every 14 days all spring and summer with liquid houseplant food diluted to maker's instructions (see p.8).
Soil: Ericaceous peat mixture (acid) or equal quantities brown fibrous peat, well decayed leaf soil and sand.
Repotting: Once every 2 years in early autumn, immediately after new growth has taken place, but before buds are fully formed. Put plenty of crocks in bottom of pot.
Cleaning: Spray with soft, tepid water weekly for cleaning and humidity except when in flower. Use leafshine every 4 weeks if necessary, being careful to avoid flowers and buds.

Camellias have attractive evergreen leaves and produce buds in winter for early spring flowering. The flowers are usually symmetrical and of striking colours including red, pink, and white.

Webs under leaves. Red spider mite. Remove webs with damp cloth or sponge, then spray with diluted malathion, especially under leaves. Repeat every 14 days until symptoms disappear. Improve humidity by standing pot on saucer of pebbles almost covered in water and spray with water regularly.

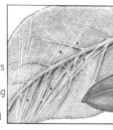

what goes wrong

Leaves dusty. Needs cleaning. Use leafshine not more than once a month. Avoid flowers when spraying water or leafshine.

Leaves fall in winter. Some leaves drop naturally, part of plant's normal development.

Plant grows throughout winter. If this happens, no flower buds will appear. Too hot, air too dry. Keep at maximum 55°F (13°C) in winter, with humid atmosphere. Spray every week with soft tepid water and stand pot on wet pebbles.

Leaves small, no flower buds appear. Needs feeding. Feed with houseplant food diluted to maker's recommended strength every 14 days in growing season, spring and summer.

Leaves turn pale green. Lime damage. Use only soft water to water and spray plant. Feed immediately with sequestered iron. Use lime-free (ericaceous) compost when repotting.

Humidity

Spray every week all year round with soft, tepid water. Protect flowers. For extra humidity, stand pot on saucer of pebbles. Add water to almost cover pebbles but do not let base of pot touch the water or the roots will become waterlogged.

Flowers turn translucent. Leafshine damage. Protect flowers from leafshine when spraying.

Discs on leaves. Scale insect, common in camellias. Spray underside of leaves with diluted malathion and, after 48 hours, remove discs with thumbnail. Repeat every week for 4 weeks until clear.

Leaves dry out. Damage by sunlight. Move into an area of diffused daylight, out of harmful rays of sun. Remove damaged leaf.

Leaves droop and turn yellow. Too wet, waterlogged. In spring, autumn and winter keep moist but well drained. Do not stand in water. In summer allow surface of compost to dry out between waterings until buds have fully formed; once a week is probably enough to keep it correct.

Buds fall off without opening. Lime damage. Feed immediately with sequestered iron and use only soft water for watering and spraying plant. Use lime-free compost when repotting.

Compost dries out and will not absorb water. Rootball very compact. Too dry, plunge pot into bucket of water for 10-15 minutes, then drain. Keep compost constantly moist in spring, autumn and winter, watering at least twice a week. In summer allow surface to dry out between waterings, until buds are fully formed.

Ornamental chilli pepper

This plant belongs to the same family of peppers which produces, when the fruits are dried, cayenne pepper and paprika. The oval fruits are edible. They can be allowed to hang on the plant for about two weeks once they are ripe. The flowers are white, with an occasional greenish tinge, and are insignificant compared with the fruit, which starts life yellow and ripens into bright red. Ornamental chilli peppers will grow in a temperature as low as 50°F (10°C) and are therefore well suited to a house without central heating.

Ornamental chilli peppers are grown principally for the autumn colour of their fruit which ripens from yellow to a bright red. The small white flowers appear in early summe The fruits can be eaten but are very hot.

Light: Full light, including sunlight.
Temperature: Between 50°F (10°C) and 70°F (21°C) all year round.
Water: Daily in spring and summer, but pot should not stand in water. When flowers have set and fruit is forming reduce watering to once a week.
Humidity: Spray daily with soft, tepid water. (This also helps to control red spider.) After flowering, spray twice weekly until fruit begins to form.
Feeding: Weekly with liquid houseplant food diluted to maker's instructions (see p.8) from spring and summer until fruit forms, then do not feed again until following season.
Soil: Loam-based No.1.
Repotting: In early spring into pot of maximum 5in (13cm) size. Plant produces more flowers and fruit if roots are slightly crowded in pot. Put plenty of broken crocks in bottom of pot: good drainage is essential.
Cleaning: Humidity spraying sufficient. No leafshine.

Spraying
Regular spraying with soft tepid water provides humidity, helps to control red spider mite and helps the fruit to set. After flowering spray twice weekly until fruit forms.

Leaves grow lush but no flowers appear. Pot too large. Plant flowers better when slightly pot bound. Do not repot for two years.

Leaves pale, no fruit or flowers. Needs feeding. Feed with liquid houseplant food every 7 days in spring and summer until fruit has formed.

what goes wrong

Plant does not grow. Too cold. Move to warmer place and do not allow temperature to fall below 50°F (10°C).

Stems grow long and lanky. Too hot. Move to a cooler place with more ventilation. Spray daily with soft, tepid water. Maximum temperature 70°F (21°C). Prune in spring, cutting back stems to within 2in (5cm) of pot.

New leaves distorted and sticky with green insects. Greenfly. Spray with pyrethrum-based insecticide or diluted malathion. Repeat one week later, then every week until clear.

Fruit does not turn from yellow to red. Too dark. Move to position in very good light. Plant will stand direct sunshine but make sure compost does not dry out when in full sun.

Leaves yellow with webs underneath. Red spider mite. Remove webs with damp cloth or sponge, then spray with diluted malathion, especially under leaves. Repeat every 14 days until symptoms disappear. Improve humidity by standing pot on saucer of wet pebbles, and spraying regularly with soft, tepid water.

All leaves turn yellow and drop. Too hot or plant waterlogged, standing in water. Check conditions. Move to place with good ventilation and temperature not more than 70°F (21°C). If compost heavy and damp, drain away any water from saucer and allow surface to dry out before watering again. Always throw away excess that drains through after watering.

Leaves turn black. Too cold or leafshine damage. Move to position where temperature at least 50°F (10°C). Do not use leafshine: clean by spraying with water.

Leaves turn yellow. Compost too dry. Water immediately, then water daily to keep compost moist in spring and summer. After fruit has set in winter water less often, only once a week.

Flies hopping around plant. Whitefly. Spray weekly until clear with pyrethrum-based insecticide or diluted malathion.

Leaves wilt and drop. Too dark. Move to position in good light. Plant will stand full sunlight.

39

Chrysanthemum

This is the national flower of Japan, the country from which it originates. The Chrysanthemum varieties sold as pot plants are commercially grown all year round and treated with growth retardant to keep a compact shape. If planted in the garden after flowering, they will lose their compactness. Plants should always be bought with their buds showing colour, as tight-budded plants are unlikely to open in the home. They should be kept on the cool side, and their dead flowers removed as they occur. Both single and double varieties are available in a range of colours.

Light: Full light including sun but avoiding direct sunshine at midday.

Temperature: Best at 60°F (16°C) all year round, although will tolerate up to 70°F (21°C) for short periods if humidity is high.

Water: About twice a week all year round to keep compost evenly moist, but do not stand pot in water. Water just as surface begins to dry.

Humidity: Spray lightly once a week in centrally heated rooms, avoiding flowers. Using soft water will prevent lime spots from forming on leaves. Do not keep in very humid situations, as leaves will quickly turn yellow.

Feeding: Not necessary if bought in bud.

Soil: Equal parts loam-based No.2, peat and sand.

Repotting: Not necessary as plant is usually thrown away once flowering has finished. The roots can be planted into a cool greenhouse, but plant will revert to full size in the following season, when specialist knowledge in chrysanthemum techniques of disbudding and culture are needed for success.

Cleaning: Humidity spraying sufficient. No leafshine.

Chrysanthemums are among the most popular flowering houseplants and are available all the year round. Look for plants with buds that have begun to open. Keep out of very humid situations or the leaves will quickly turn yellow.

Flowers rot when leaves healthy and all conditions correct. Flower has been sprayed. When spraying with water or insecticide, shield flowers with your hand or paper. Remove damaged flower head.

Leaves turn black. Too cold. Move to warmer place, keep at 60°F (16°C) all year round. If temperature correct, leafshine damage. Do not use. Clean only by spraying with soft tepid water (avoiding flowers). Remove damaged leaf.

Leaves and stems shrivel up. Too hot. Move to a cooler place with more ventilation. Ideal temperature 60°F (16°C) all year round. Spray weekly with soft, tepid water, shielding flowers from spray.

Lower leaves turn black. Botrytis. Too cold and damp. Spray with fungicide then place in warmer position and spray with water less often. Allow compost almost to dry out on surface between waterings. Minimum temperature 60°F (16°C) all year round. Remove damaged leaves.

Removing dead flowers and leaves

1. When flower heads die, cut them off cleanly at point where flower stalk joins main stem.

2. Damaged or dead leaves should be cut off in the same way, where leaf stalk joins main stem.

Many small buds do not open. Insufficient light. Move to sunny position and rub off some of the smaller buds to encourage stronger ones to grow. Allow up to 5 buds per flower stem.

what goes wrong

Flower buds dry out and do not open. Compost too dry. Plunge pot into bucket of water for 10–15 minutes, then drain. Keep constantly moist in summer, watering every day if it dries out in hot weather. Do not allow to stand in water.

Plant grows long stems with lanky leaves. Insufficient light. Move to place in very good light. It will stand direct sunlight except at midday.

Leaves turn yellow. Atmosphere too humid. Move to drier position and do not spray, unless in dry centrally heated room.

Webs on flowers and leaves. Red spider mite. Remove webs with damp cloth or sponge, then spray with diluted malathion, especially under leaves. Repeat every 14 days until symptoms disappear. Improve humidity by spraying lightly once a week in centrally heated rooms.

Flies hopping around plant. Whitefly, chrysanthemum fly or blackfly. Spray with pyrethrum-based insecticide or diluted malathion. Repeat one week later then every week until clear. This is very common.

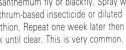

41

Clerodendrum thomsonae

Bleeding heart vine

These plants come mainly from Africa and Malaysia and are supposed to have a wide range of medicinal properties. Some varieties are hardy, but this one must be kept at a temperature of at least 55°F (13°C) if it is to survive. Plants sold in flower shops are usually sprayed with growth retardant to help keep them compact and producing abundant flowers. The unusual flowers are dark red, offset by creamy-white bracts. The foliage appears strong and glossy but is susceptible to damage by leafshine and will soon rot if too cold. Pruning the plant down to 3in (7cm) after flowering is over will encourage healthy growth in the following year.

The Bleeding heart vine is a naturally lanky plant which should be kept compact by heavy pruning after flowering. The cream-coloured bracts are strikingly shaped and have contrasting dark red centre. They may appear at any time from spring to early autumn.

Light: Full light, including sunshine, but avoid midday summer sun.

Temperature: 65–70°F (18–21°C) from spring to late autumn; 55–60°F (13–16°C) late autumn to spring.

Water: Twice weekly from mid-spring to later summer to keep always moist, weekly from late summer to end autumn, then only when compost has almost dried out. Once a fortnight probably enough.

Humidity: Needs high humidity. Greenhouse conditions ideal. In the home, spray twice weekly from spring to end summer. Stand pot on a saucer of pebbles almost covered with water.

Feeding: Weekly with liquid houseplant food diluted to maker's instructions (see p.8) from spring to end summer. Do not feed in winter.

Soil: Equal parts loam-based No. 2, peat, leafmould and sand.

Repotting: In early spring. Prune the plant in autumn, after flowering has finished, down to about 3in(7cm).

Cleaning: Humidity spraying with soft tepid water sufficient. No leafshine.

Humidity

Bleeding heart vines need high humidity, especially in warm weather. Spray twice a week in spring and summer and stand pot on saucer of pebbles almost covered with water. Do not allow pot base to touch water.

Pruning

Prune plant after flowers have died. Cut stem at an angle just above leaf, leaving about 3in (7½cm) stem above compost. Cut cleanly with sharp secateurs.

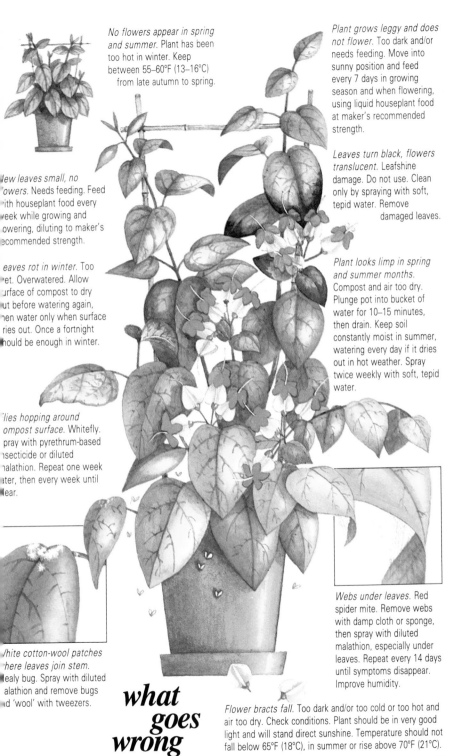

No flowers appear in spring and summer. Plant has been too hot in winter. Keep between 55–60°F (13–16°C) from late autumn to spring.

Plant grows leggy and does not flower. Too dark and/or needs feeding. Move into sunny position and feed every 7 days in growing season and when flowering, using liquid houseplant food at maker's recommended strength.

Leaves turn black, flowers translucent. Leafshine damage. Do not use. Clean only by spraying with soft, tepid water. Remove damaged leaves.

New leaves small, no flowers. Needs feeding. Feed with houseplant food every week while growing and flowering, diluting to maker's recommended strength.

Leaves rot in winter. Too wet. Overwatered. Allow surface of compost to dry out before watering again, then water only when surface dries out. Once a fortnight should be enough in winter.

Plant looks limp in spring and summer months. Compost and air too dry. Plunge pot into bucket of water for 10–15 minutes, then drain. Keep soil constantly moist in summer, watering every day if it dries out in hot weather. Spray twice weekly with soft, tepid water.

Flies hopping around compost surface. Whitefly. Spray with pyrethrum-based insecticide or diluted malathion. Repeat one week later, then every week until clear.

White cotton-wool patches where leaves join stem. Mealy bug. Spray with diluted malathion and remove bugs and 'wool' with tweezers.

Webs under leaves. Red spider mite. Remove webs with damp cloth or sponge, then spray with diluted malathion, especially under leaves. Repeat every 14 days until symptoms disappear. Improve humidity.

what goes wrong

Flower bracts fall. Too dark and/or too cold or too hot and air too dry. Check conditions. Plant should be in very good light and will stand direct sunshine. Temperature should not fall below 65°F (18°C), in summer or rise above 70°F (21°C).

43

Goldfish plant

This is a spectacular flowering plant which looks at its best in a hanging basket. In spring it produces a succession of bright orange flowers down the length of its hanging stems. Viewed from the side, the flowers look like leaping fish. In its natural habitat, the goldfish plant grows on trees or dead wood, but the roots merely support the plant and do not take their nourishment from the host. When grown in baskets, however, the plants do benefit from feeding.

Light: Full diffused daylight (see p.12) but avoid direct sunshine.

Temperature: 55–60°F (13–16°C) is best, if possible. Temperatures up to 75°F (24°C) can be tolerated if humidity is high.

Water: At least twice weekly in summer to keep compost constantly moist, though plant must not stand in water. Reduce to weekly watering in autumn; and in winter, only after surface has quite dried out – in practice, about once every 10 days.

Humidity: Spray daily with soft water in spring and summer to maintain high humidity, especially if temperature over 60°F (16°C). Avoid spraying flowers. Stand pot on saucer of pebbles almost covered with water; with a hanging basket, keep water in drip tray.

Feeding: Use liquid houseplant food every 14 days in spring and summer, diluted to maker's instructions (see p.8).

Soil: 3 parts loam-based No.1 with 1 part extra peat added.

Repotting: Only every 2 or 3 years, in late spring. If replanting a hanging basket, remove chains first, being careful not to damage the long trailing stems. Put plenty of crocks in bottom of pot or basket.

Cleaning: Humidity spraying adequate. No leafshine.

Another variety of Goldfish plant is *Columnea gloriosa* which has larger leaves than *C. microphylla* but very similar blooms. Like the smaller-leaved plant, it has striking red flowers which appear among its trailing stems.

White cotton-wool patches at base of leaves. Mealy bug. Spray with diluted malathion and remove bugs and 'wool' with tweezers. Repeat every 14 days until symptoms disappear. Or, paint bugs with methylated spirits and remove with tweezers.

Humidity

1. Spray plants in hanging baskets every day in spring and summer, as they dry out quickly.
2. To provide constant humidity, hang a drip tray under the basket and keep it half filled with water. Humidity will rise around the plant as the water evaporates.

eaves drop, stem starts to ot. Too cold and/or too wet. 1ove to warmer place, at ast 55°F (13°C). Check ompost is not waterlogged. rain away any excess water om saucer and allow surface f compost to dry out before atering again. Never allow ot to stand in water.

Leaves turn black, flowers transparent. Leafshine damage. Do not use. Clean only by spraying with soft, tepid water but do not allow even water on the flowers.

Tips of stems shrivel, in summer then all leaves. Compost too dry. Plunge pot into bucket of water for 10–15 minutes, then drain. Keep constantly moist in summer, watering at least twice a week. Do not allow to stand in water. Spray daily with soft, tepid water.

Scorch marks on flowers. Too much direct sunlight. Keep in good diffused light, not sunlight.

Leaves healthy but no flowers appear. Not enough light. Move to position in diffused daylight but not direct sun. If new leaves small, also needs feeding. Feed every 2 weeks in spring and summer.

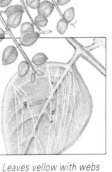

Leaves yellow with webs underneath. Red spider mite. Remove webs with damp cloth or sponge, then spray with diluted malathion, especially under leaves. Repeat every 14 days until symptoms disappear. Improve humidity by regular spraying with soft tepid water.

eaves dry, plant looks ull. Air too dry. Spray daily ith soft tepid water in spring nd summer. Provide extra umidity by standing pot on aucer of wet pebbles. Do ot position hanging baskets ver radiators.

tems straggly with long spaces between aves. Needs feeding. Feed with houseplant od at recommended strength every 2 eeks in spring and summer.

what goes wrong

Leaves turn brown and no flowers appear. Too hot. Move to cooler place with more ventilation. Spray daily with soft, tepid water. Maximum temperature 75°F (24°C).

45

Firecracker flower

Although a bit tricky to keep, with correct care the Firecracker flower can be made to bloom almost continuously from spring to late summer. The plant prefers a dry atmosphere and will rot if too humid. It has orange flowers growing from green bracts not unlike ears of corn; the dark green glossy leaves are attractive but deceptively tender. The plant can be easily increased by taking cuttings at almost any time of year and rooting them in sand. Newly bought plants should have shiny leaves with no black marks anywhere.

The Firecracker flower's blooms are produced from late spring onwards, and make a strongly coloured contrast to the lush foliage. The leaves look glossy and strong but wilt rapidly if they become wet. A good plant for a dry atmosphere.

Light: Shade from direct light in spring and summer; in winter, give full daylight including sunshine.

Temperature: Best at 65°F (18°C) all year round, with summer maximum of 70°F (21°C) if kept very dry.

Water: Only when compost surface dry, using tepid soft water. This applies all year round and probably means once a week in summer, once every 10 days in winter, depending on the temperature. Avoid getting water on the leaves; never stand plant in water. Overwatering will kill this plant.

Humidity: Atmosphere must be dry with a good circulation of air. In very hot weather (over 70°F, 21°C), stand pot on saucer of pebbles almost covered with water. Never spray plant or keep in humid greenhouse.

Feeding: Weekly during growing period only with liquid houseplant food diluted to maker's instructions (see p.8).

Soil: 2 parts loam-based No. 2 and 1 part added sand.

Repotting: In early spring into pot with plenty of broken crocks in bottom for good spraying, no leafshine.

Flowers and leaves rot. Botrytis. Plant too cold and damp. Spray with fungicide following maker's instructions, then place in warmer position, at least 55°F (13°C) in winter, 65°F (18°C) in summer. Always allow surface to dry out between waterings. Remove damaged leaves and flowers.

Leaves curl up and edges turn black. Compost too moist and too much humidity. Allow surface of soil to dry out before watering again, then water only after surface dries out each time. Once a week in summer, once every 10 days in winter should be enough. Do not spray.

Removing flowers

Flowers open and fall progressively, from base of flower spike. Remove dead ones as they fall. When all have died, cut off flower stem just above the topmost pair of leaves.

anky growth, no flowers.
oo dark. Move to lighter
lace, will take full sun in
vinter.

Flowers turn translucent.
Plant has been sprayed with
water. Do not spray. Provide
humidity by standing pot on
saucer of wet pebbles if
temperature over 70°F (21°C).

Plant does not grow. Too
cold. Move to warmer place,
at least 55°F (13°C) in winter;
65°F (18°C) in summer.

what goes wrong

Many leaves turn black all
over. Too cold. Move to
warmer place. Do not allow
temperature to drop below
55°F (13°C) in winter; best
between 65°F (18°C) and
70°F (21°C) in summer. Or,
leafshine damage.

New leaves small in spring.
Needs feeding. Feed weekly
in spring and summer with
houseplant food diluted to
recommended strength.

Leaves shrivel and turn
brown. Too hot and dry, air
too dry. Water if surface of
compost has dried out and
move to cooler position,
under 70° (21°C) if possible.
Do not spray, but provide
extra humidity by standing
pot on saucer of wet pebbles.

Leaves develop brown
spots, plant wilts and
collapses. Gas fumes. Move
to fume-free room.

Webs under leaves. Red
spider mite. Remove webs
with a dry cloth and add
systemic insecticide such as
malathion to water for
compost. Do not spray with
insecticide. Repeat treatment
after 10 days if pest persists.
Improve humidity by standing
pot on wet pebbles.

eaves go limp. Compost too moist and/or
a cold draught. Allow surface to dry out
etween waterings – once a week in summer,
nce every 10 days in winter should be
nough. Move plant out of draughts.

Some flower petals fall from flower spike. Natural. Flowers
appear and fade progressively from the bottom of the spike
to the top.

Cytisus canariensis

Madeira Broom

This plant (also known as Florist's genista) is almost hardy and should be kept in cool situations but protected from frost. It dislikes central heating but will tolerate temperatures of up to 65°F (18°C) if there is good ventilation. It is ideally suited to the unheated greenhouse or to a glassed porch or sun-room extension. Its yellow pea-shaped flowers grow from pale green, fresh-looking foliage which has three leaflets to every leaf and grows on up-right stems. After flowering, the plant should be pruned to half its height to encourage a compact plant of good shape the following year. The plant usually loses its leaves in winter.

The Madeira broom, or the Florist's genista is almost hardy and produces its bright yellow flowers in summer. Keep cool (55–60°F, 13–16°C) and water well when hot. The fresh green foliage makes it an attractive spring foliage plant but it is usually sold when in flower.

Light: Full light, avoiding midday sun in summer.
Temperature: Maintain 55–60°F (13–16°C) although plant will tolerate 65°F (18°C) if ventilation good. Winter minimum is 40°F (4°C).
Water: Twice weekly in spring and summer, to keep moist but plant must not stand in water. In winter, water only when compost surface has dried out, about once every 10 days.
Humidity: Spray daily in temperatures above 60°F (16°C). Otherwise, twice weekly in spring and summer. Do not spray in winter.
Feeding: Every 14 days in spring and summer with houseplant food diluted to half maker's recommended strength (see p.8). Do not feed in winter.
Soil: 2 parts loam-based No. 3 to 1 part sand to make light, well-drained compost.
Repotting: In spring with plenty of broken crocks in bottom of pot for good drainage.
Cleaning: Humidity spraying with soft water adequate. No leafshine.

Leaves pale. Not enough light. Move to a position in good light but not midday summer sun.

what goes wrong

Pruning

1. Prune stems when flowers have died, cutting them down to half their length. If not pruned, plants grow straggly and out of shape.

2. Cut stem cleanly with sharp secateurs, cutting just above a leaf. Cut at an angle as shown. Dab cut ends with sulphur dust and if sap runs, seal ends with petroleum jelly.

Leaves and stems grow quickly and outgrow pot. Needs pruning. Should have been pruned after flowering to encourage good flowers the following year. Next year prune when flowering is over.

Whole plant flops when compost moist. Too wet, waterlogged; may be standing in water. Drain away any water in saucer and allow surface of compost to dry out before watering again. Keep moist in spring and summer but never allow pot base to stand in water. Always throw away excess that drains through after watering. In winter allow surface to dry out between waterings.

Leaves dry out, flowers fade rapidly. Too hot and air too dry. Move to cooler place with more ventilation and spray daily with soft, tepid water. Maximum temperature in summer 60–65°F (16–18°C). Provide extra humidity by standing pot on saucer of wet pebbles.

Flies hopping around plant. Whitefly. Spray with pyrethrum-based insecticide or diluted malathion. Repeat one week later, then every week until clear.

Flowers fall as soon as they form. Too hot. Move to cooler place with more ventilation, not more than 65°F (18°C) in summer. Spray daily with soft, tepid water.

Leaves turn black. Too cold, frost damage. Keep above 40°F (4°C) in winter, away from cold windows. In winter allow compost surface to dry out more between waterings: once every 10 days is probably enough.

Leaves dry and drop. Soil much too dry. Water immediately and keep compost always moist in spring and summer, watering once or twice a week. In winter keep drier, watering about once every 10 days.

Leaf tips very small, flower buds fall. Needs feeding. Feed with houseplant food every 14 days in spring and summer. Dilute food to half maker's recommended strength.

49

Dipladenia sanderi

Pink allamande

This climbing plant produces pairs of pale green leaves along the length of a fairly fast-growing stem. It can be trained round a loop of wire or up a trellis. The trumpet-shaped flowers are salmon pink with a yellow centre. The plant needs high humidity, which also helps to control red spider mite, to which it is particularly susceptible. It should be pruned hard annually after flowering to keep it compact. Propagation is by cuttings of the young shoots which appear when the plant begins to grow in spring. The shoots will soon root if kept in a warm (65°F, 18°C) humid atmosphere in a compost of equal parts of sand and peat.

The Pink allamande is a vigorous climber which flowers in summer. A trellis or cane will be required to train it and keep it under control, although it is well suited to training round a hoop. Watch for red spider mite, to which they are particularly susceptible.

Light: Full light, including sunlight except midday sun in summer.
Temperature: Average 65°F (18°C) in summer, and 60°F (16°C) in winter, not more than 70°F (21°C), not less than 55°F (13°C).
Water: 2 or 3 times a week in summer to keep moist, but plant must not stand in water or become waterlogged. In winter, water only when top layer of compost feels completely dry, about every 10 days.
Humidity: Spray daily in spring and summer. Stand pot on saucer of pebbles almost covered with water all year round, or plunge into an outer pot, with damp peat between the pots.
Feeding: Every 14 days in spring and summer with liquid houseplant food diluted to half maker's instructions (see p.8).
Soil: 4 parts rough, fibrous peat and 1 part silver sand.
Repotting: In the first year, repot into next sized pot every time roots grow through bottom of pot. In subsequent years change top soil only.
Cleaning: Humidity spraying adequate. No leafshine.

Plant looks dull and lifeless, especially on warm days. Air too dry. Spray daily with soft tepid water. Provide extra humidity by standing pot on saucer of damp pebbles.

Plant flops. Too cold and wet. Allow top layer of compost to dry out before watering again and move to warmer position, at least 55°F (13°C).

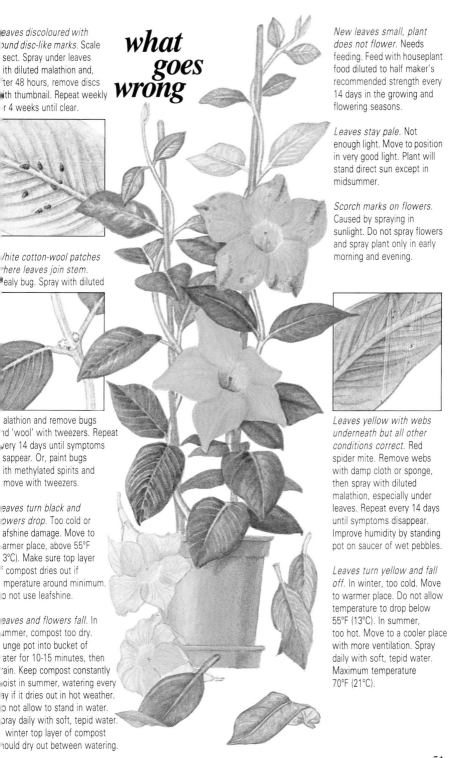

what goes wrong

eaves discoloured with
ound disc-like marks. Scale
sect. Spray under leaves
ith diluted malathion and,
ter 48 hours, remove discs
ith thumbnail. Repeat weekly
r 4 weeks until clear.

/hite cotton-wool patches
here leaves join stem.
ealy bug. Spray with diluted

alathion and remove bugs
nd 'wool' with tweezers. Repeat
very 14 days until symptoms
sappear. Or, paint bugs
ith methylated spirits and
move with tweezers.

eaves turn black and
owers drop. Too cold or
afshine damage. Move to
armer place, above 55°F
3°C). Make sure top layer
compost dries out if
mperature around minimum.
o not use leafshine.

eaves and flowers fall. In
immer, compost too dry.
unge pot into bucket of
ater for 10-15 minutes, then
rain. Keep compost constantly
oist in summer, watering every
ay if it dries out in hot weather.
o not allow to stand in water.
oray daily with soft, tepid water.
winter top layer of compost
ould dry out between watering.

New leaves small, plant
does not flower. Needs
feeding. Feed with houseplant
food diluted to half maker's
recommended strength every
14 days in the growing and
flowering seasons.

Leaves stay pale. Not
enough light. Move to position
in very good light. Plant will
stand direct sun except in
midsummer.

Scorch marks on flowers.
Caused by spraying in
sunlight. Do not spray flowers
and spray plant only in early
morning and evening.

Leaves yellow with webs
underneath but all other
conditions correct. Red
spider mite. Remove webs
with damp cloth or sponge,
then spray with diluted
malathion, especially under
leaves. Repeat every 14 days
until symptoms disappear.
Improve humidity by standing
pot on saucer of wet pebbles.

Leaves turn yellow and fall
off. In winter, too cold. Move
to warmer place. Do not allow
temperature to drop below
55°F (13°C). In summer,
too hot. Move to a cooler place
with more ventilation. Spray
daily with soft, tepid water.
Maximum temperature
70°F (21°C).

51

Fuchsia

Named after Leonard Fuchs, a six-teenth-century German botanical writer, Fuchsias originate in Central and South America. The flowers range from pale pink to dark red and purple in colour. Usually, they are given a resting period in winter, when they should be placed in a cool, light situation with a minimum temperature of 45°F (7°C). When the plant is growing, the side tips should be pinched out every 2 weeks to make it bushy.

New varieties of Fuchsia appear almost every year in a great number of different colours. Plants are always sold in flower, at a height of about 12–15in (30–38cm) and should be kept in a cool light place.

Light: Bright light, including full sun, but not midday summer sunlight.

Temperature: Summer maximum 60°F (16°C), though tolerates 65°F (18°C) if humidity is very high. Winter 45-50°F (7-10°C), to rest until early spring.

Water: Moderately, just as surface begins to dry out – weekly in spring, twice weekly in summer. After flowering, reduce water to weekly again. In winter, allow soil surface to dry out completely between waterings. Every 14 days sufficient.

Humidity: Spray with soft water twice weekly in spring and twice daily in summer, especially in very hot weather. Spray twice weekly in late summer, and stop altogether in autumn and winter.

Feeding: As soon as flower buds appear feed weekly with liquid houseplant food diluted to maker's instructions (see p.8). Stop feeding in late summer.

Soil: 1 part loam-based No. 2, 1 part peat, 1 part decayed manure, 1 part leafmould and sand.

Repotting: Early in spring, after pruning back to woody part of stem, to conserve compact shape. Use pot 2 sizes larger for first 2 years, as plants with prolific roots will flower more profusely.

Cleaning: Humidity spraying adequate. No leafshine.

Leaves turn black. Leafshine damage. Do not use. Clean by spraying with water or, in winter, with feather duster if dusty.

Buds do not develop; flowers fade quickly. Too hot. Keep as cool as possible in summer, not more than 65°F (18°C) best, but not below 45°F (7°C).

what goes wrong

Buds, then open flowers and leaves drop. Air too dry or too dark. In hot weather spray twice daily with water and stand pot on saucer of wet pebbles. Move into lighter place.

New leaves small, no flowers. Needs feeding. Feed with houseplant food every week in summer, as soon as buds appear. Dilute food to recommended strength.

Leaves turn yellow and droop. Too wet, waterlogged. Allow compost surface to dry out before watering again. Check drainage hole in pot. Never allow pot to stand in water.

Bulbous pod on flower stem. Seed pod. Remove to prolong flowering period. Propagation is easier by cuttings than from seed.

Small flies all over leaves and flower buds. Greenfly. Spray with pyrethrum-based insecticide or diluted malathion. Repeat one week later, then every week until clear.

Plant grows strongly with lots of leaves and stems but no flowers. Feeding started too soon. Do not feed until flower buds appear.

Plant grows lanky and straggly in summer, with no flowers. Too dark. Move to position in good light. Plant needs direct sun, except midday summer sun. In winter, too hot. Allow plant to rest at temperature of 45–50°F (7–10°C).

Leaves droop. Too dry. Water immediately and spray leaves. In spring and summer, water when compost surface begins to dry out, watering once or twice a week. In winter, keep drier.

White cotton-wool patches where leaves join stem. Mealy bug. Spray with diluted malathion and remove bugs and 'wool' with tweezers. Repeat every 14 days until symptoms disappear. Or, paint bugs with methylated spirits and remove with tweezers.

White patches on leaves. Damage caused by spraying in sunlight. Plant needs high humidity but must not be sprayed when sun is shining on it.

Stems stay green in autumn/winter. Too wet and too hot. Reduce watering to once every 14 days to ripen wood and keep plant at 45–50°F (7–10°C) for resting period in winter.

Leaves fall in winter. Too cold. Keep between 45–50° (7–10°C) in winter, allowing compost surface to dry out.

53

Gardenia jasminoides

Cape jasmine

This outstanding flowering plant may be difficult to keep in the home, but its almost porcelain-like flowers with their beautiful fragrance make it rewarding. The pure white flowers are offset by glossy, thick, dark green leaves. Gardenias are lime-hating and should be watered with soft water only and planted in lime-free compost. A relatively high temperature and humidity are essential to prolong the flowering period in spring and summer.

Light: Full daylight, avoiding direct midday summer sun.

Temperature: 65-70°F (18-21°C) all spring and summer. Tolerates up to 75°F (24°C) if humidity high. Winter minimum 50°F (10°C).

Water: 2 or 3 times a week in spring and summer, once a week in autumn and winter, to allow surface to dry out a little. Use tepid, soft water only.

Humidity: Spray daily in spring and summer with soft water, avoiding flowers or buds. Stand pot on saucer of pebbles almost covered with water to maintain high humidity. Avoid centrally heated rooms unless there is a humidifier.

Feeding: Water with sequestered iron once in early spring and once again in summer. Then feed every 2 weeks with liquid houseplant food diluted to half maker's instructions (see p.8) until autumn.

Soil: Acid mixture using ericaceous peat blended half and half with lime-free loam.

Repotting: In early spring for first 3 years, into pot one size larger each time. Then repot only if root ball is compact, up to a maximum pot size 7in (18cm). After this, just change top soil.

Cleaning: Humidity spraying adequate. Vegetable oil-based leafshine may be used on leaves every 2 months.

The Gardinia's glossy, dark green leaves are a perfect foil for its beautiful, highly scented, pure white flowers. Buds often drop infuriatingly just as they are about to open. This is caused by a combination of lime damage, insufficient humidity and too low a temperature.

Flowers discoloured. Damage from water spray. Protect flowers when spraying.

what goes wrong

Leaves turn black in winter. Too cold. Move to warmer place and do not allow temperature to drop below 50°F (10°C).

Leaves pale. Too dark. Move to position in full daylight but not in direct midday sun.

Webs under leaves. Red spider mite. Remove webs with damp cloth or sponge, then spray with diluted malathion, especially under leaves. Repeat every 14 days until symptoms disappear. Improve humidity by standing pot on saucer of wet pebbles.

Humidity

Gardenias need high humidity, especially in spring and summer. Spray every day with soft water, protecting flowers and buds. Stand pot on saucer of pebbles almost covered in water but don't let the pot base touch the water or roots will be waterlogged.

Plant does not flower. Air too dry. Spray leaves daily with soft tepid water and provide extra humidity by standing pot on saucer of damp pebbles. When flowers appear, be careful to keep water off them, but continue spraying leaves.

Plant flops, buds drop. Too cold and wet. Allow compost surface to dry out before watering again and increase temperature to at least 60°F (16°C). As temperature rises, provide extra humidity by spraying and standing pot on damp pebbles.

New leaves small. Needs feeding. Feed every 14 days with houseplant food diluted to half maker's recommended strength. Add sequestered iron to the water once in spring and once in summer, following instructions on bottle.

Leaves discoloured with round discs. Scale insect. Spray underside of leaves with diluted malathion and, after 48 hours, remove discs with thumbnail. Repeat every week for 4 weeks until clear.

Scorch marks on leaves and flowers. Sprayed in sunlight. Spray only in early morning or evening.

Leaves turn yellow, while veins remain green. Lime damage from hard water or incorrect compost. Water with sequestered iron once in spring, following directions on bottle and once in summer. Use only soft water for watering and spraying. Repot in early spring in lime-free compost.

Flowers turn yellow. Humidity too high. Improve ventilation around plant but keep temperature at least 60–65°F (16–18°C) in summer, 50°F (10°C) in winter and do not allow humidity to fall too much or buds will drop.

White cotton-wool patches where leaves join stem. Mealy bug. Spray with diluted malathion and remove bugs and 'wool' with tweezers. Repeat every 14 days until symptoms disappear. Or, paint bugs with methylated spirits and remove with tweezers.

Flower buds drop on healthy plant. Lime in tap water or lack of humidity. Use soft water for watering and spraying and keep humidity and temperature up in summer. Needs summer temperature of 65–70°F (18–21°C).

Leaves fall off in summer. Compost too dry. Plunge pot into bucket of water for 10–15 minutes, then drain. Keep constantly moist in summer, watering every day if it dries out in hot weather, but do not allow to stand in water.

Guzmania lingulata

Scarlet star

In its natural habitat, South America and the West Indies, this plant is usually found growing in the boughs of trees; the out-stretched leaves gather such little rain as falls into a well-shaped centre from which the flower bract grows. The strap-shaped leaves tend to lose some of their colour as the bracts develop, but the bracts themselves are wine-red and last for up to eight weeks. Small pale yellow flowers will emerge from the bract after about eight weeks. Like all Bromeliads (see p.30) it flowers only once in its 3-year lifespan, then produces offsets from its base.

Scarlet stars produce wine-coloured bracts from which small yellow flowers appear. This is one of many varieties of *Guzmania*, all of which require the same conditions of temperature, humidity and watering.

Light: Full diffused daylight all year round (see p.12). No direct sunlight.

Temperature: Maintain 60–70°F (16–21°C) in spring and summer. Plant tolerates winter temperature as low as 55°F (13°C), provided humidity is also low.

Water: Keep moist in spring and summer by filling central well, once or twice a week, allowing water to overflow into compost. In winter, water only when surface feels dry and well is empty. Always use soft water.

Humidity: Spray daily when temperature near maximum but plant is tolerant; needs plenty of air around it. Very high humidity and low temperatures can lead to botrytis.

Feeding: Once in spring using liquid house-plant food diluted to a quarter of maker's instructions (see p.8). Water into the well.

Soil: Equal parts lime-free loam and peat.

Repotting: When offsets develop. Wait until parent plant has dried up, then repot offset.

Cleaning: Every 2 months wipe leaves with vegetable oil-based leafshine. If dusty at other times wipe with damp sponge. Do not spray bracts.

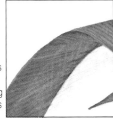

Webs under leaves. Red spider mite. Remove webs with damp cloth or sponge, then spray with diluted malathion, especially under leaves. Repeat every 14 days until symptoms disappear. Improve humidity by standing pot on saucer of wet pebbles or in outer pot packed with peat.

Watering

Fill plant's central well with soft water and allow it to spill over onto compost. Keep compost moist in summer, watering twice a week in hot weather. In winter wait until well is empty and compost surface feels dry.

what goes wrong

Parent plant dies as side shoot develops. Natural after 3 years. Wait until parent plant has died, then carefully remove shoot and pot separately in mixture of sphagnum moss and peat.

Plant turns black in winter. Too cold. If also rotting at base, waterlogged. Move to warmer place, at least 55°F (13°C) and allow compost surface to dry out before watering again.

No flowers emerge from spike. Too cold and air too dry; or too dark; or needs feeding. Check conditions. Move to warmer place, between 60–70°F (16–21°C) and improve humidity by spraying with soft, tepid water. Move to light position: plant will stand full sunlight. Add food to central well once in spring, diluting it to ¼ maker's recommended strength.

Tips of leaves turn brown and dry, plant shrivels. Too hot and air too dry. Spray daily with soft tepid water when temperature near maximum and place pot in outer pot packed with damp peat. Keep under 70°F (21°C) if possible.

White marks on leaves. Caused by spraying with hard water. Use soft or rainwater for spraying.

Plant rots in summer. Botrytis – too cold and damp. Spray with fungicide then place in warmer place and spray less often. Allow compost surface to dry out between waterings. Best summer temperature between 60–70°F (16–21°C).

White cotton-wool patches round base of plant. Mealy bug. Spray with diluted malathion and remove bugs and 'wool' with tweezers. Repeat every 14 days until symptoms disappear. Or, paint bugs with methylated spirits and remove with tweezers.

Leaves brown and dry. Too dry. Keep central well filled and compost moist in summer. Allow surface to dry in winter. Always use soft water.

Lower leaves die. Too cold or, if after flowering, end of plant's life. Move to warmer place, between 60–70°F (16–21°C).

57

Hibiscus rosa – sinensis

Chinese rose

This shrubby, sub-tropical flowering plant has exotic red, yellow or orange flowers which only last one or two days before shrivelling and falling off. If the humidity is too low, the buds may fall off before opening, although a number of hybrids have been developed recently to prevent this. When buying, check that the lower buds on the plant have not dropped.

Light: Plenty of diffused light (see p.12) but never direct sun.

Temperature: 65–70°F (18–21°C), in spring and summer, with summer maximum of 80°F (27°C). Reduce to 55°F (13°C) in winter.

Water: 2 or 3 times a week in summer to maintain a moist compost, though plant must not stand in water. In winter, water only when top of compost feels dry: when temperature around 55°F (13°C), this should only be once every 14 days.

Humidity: Spray daily with soft tepid water in spring and summer. Stand pot on saucer of pebbles almost covered with water. Ensure good ventilation. In winter, spray weekly.

Feeding: Every 14 days in spring and summer, especially after flower buds appear, using liquid houseplant food diluted to maker's instructions (see p.8).

Soil: Equal parts loam-based No. 3 and peat, with one-third less peat for adult plants.

Repotting: Annually in spring into pot one size larger, up to a maximum 7in (18cm). Plant is more prolific if reasonably pot-bound. When in largest pot size, change top soil annually.

Cleaning: Humidity spraying adequate. Leaves may be wiped with a damp cloth. No leafshine.

The Hibiscus has exotic flowers which are available in red, yellow or orange; each bloom lasts only one or two days before drying out and shrivelling. Buds will fall if the humidity is too low, so spray daily with soft tepid water in spring and summer.

Flower buds fall off before opening. Air too dry. Spray daily in summer with soft, tepid water. In winter spray weekly. While growing in spring and summer, keep temperature between 65–70°F (18–21°C), to encourage buds to open.

Black marks on leaf. Leafshine damage. Do not use. Clean by spraying with soft, tepid water.

Leaves pale. Too dark. Move to lighter place, but not in direct sunlight.

Leaves drop while still green. In summer, too wet, waterlogged; roots are rotting. Check drainage holes in pot and allow soil to dry out on surface before watering again. Then water twice a week in summer to keep soil moist. In winter, too cold. Maintain 55°F (13°C) all winter. Remember to keep soil drier in winter, allowing surface layer to dry out between waterings.

what goes wrong

Pruning

Cut stems down by half in spring with secateurs or sharp scissors. Cut at an angle just above a leaf or side shoot. Dust cut ends with sulphur and if sap runs, smear ends with ash or petroleum jelly to seal the wound.

New leaves stay small, no flowers appear. Needs feeding. Feed every 2 weeks in spring and summer, using houseplant food at maker's recommended strength.

Plant wilts, leaves limp and dull. Too hot and dry. Water and move to cooler place, under 70°F (21°C) in summer, around 55°F (13°C) in winter.

Plant grows tall and straggly. Needs pruning but prune only in spring or summer. Dust pruning cuts with sulphur to prevent disease.

Leaves misshapen and sticky, with small insects. Greenfly. Spray with pyrethrum-based insecticide, or diluted malathion. Repeat 1 week later, then every week until clear.

White cotton-wool patches where leaf joins stem. Mealy bug. Spray with diluted malathion and remove bugs and 'wool' with tweezers. Repeat every 14 days until symptoms disappear. Or, paint bugs with methylated spirits and remove with tweezers.

Leaves lose shine, webs underneath. Red spider mite. Remove webs with damp cloth or sponge, then spray with diluted malathion, especially under leaves. Protect flowers. Repeat every 14 days until clear. Improve humidity. Do not restore gloss with leafshine.

Flowers fall after one day in bloom. Natural. Flowers last only a day once fully open.

59

Hoya bella

Miniature wax plant

This is a slender-stemmed plant, whose small, plain green, waxy leaves distinguish it from the larger-leaved *Hoya carnosa*. Requiring more heat than *H. carnosa*, a Miniature wax plant is ideally suited to growing in indoor hanging baskets. The flowers are a waxy white with a rose-crimson or violet centre, and they hang down in groups or clusters. The plant should not be placed on polished furniture, as the flowers produce a sticky nectar which can fall in droplets, causing damage. More popular in Victorian times, it can be difficult to obtain today, and is not easy to bring to flower, but efforts are well rewarded by the exquisite, scented blooms.

Light: Full diffused daylight (see p.12) but avoid midday sun in summer. Full sun in winter.

Temperature: 65–70°F (18–21°C) in spring and summer, though peaks of up to 85°F (30°C) will do no harm for short periods. Maintain 50°F (10°C) in winter.

Water: Weekly in spring and summer; reduce to every 14 days in autumn and winter, watering only when soil surface feels dry.

Humidity: Spray at least twice weekly with soft water in spring and summer, avoiding flowers. Planting into a hanging basket is beneficial; good ventilation important.

Feeding: Every 14 days in spring and summer only, with liquid food diluted to maker's instructions (see p.8).

Soil: Equal parts of loam-based No.2 and rough peat.

Repotting: In spring, and only when plant completely pot-bound: in practice, every 2 or 3 years.

Cleaning: Humidity spraying adequate. Wipe leaves occasionally – not more often than once every 6 weeks – with vegetable oil-based leafshine.

The Miniature wax plant's star-shaped, waxy, white flowers with a rose-crimson centre are produced at the height of summer. The flowers only measure ⅜in (1cm) but grow in clusters. Keep in temperatures of 65–70° (18–21°C) in summer, spraying twice per week in a well ventilated room.

White cotton-wool patches where leaves join stem. Mealy bug. Spray with diluted malathion and remove bugs and 'wool' with tweezers. Repeat every 14 days until symptoms disappear. Or, paint bugs with methylated spirits and remove with tweezers.

Removing flowers

When flowers die, pick off individual blooms and their flower stems. Do not remove the short side stem which carries the flower cluster. New blooms will grow from this the following year.

Flowers produce sticky nectar so protect furniture under plant while in flower.

No buds form. Too wet, overwatered. Allow surface of compost to dry out before watering again, then water only when surface feels dry. Once a week in summer, once a fortnight in winter should be enough.

what goes wrong

Leaves turn black. Too cold. Move to warmer room, not below 50°F (10°C) in winter, 65°F (18°C) in summer. Or leafshine damage.

Webs under leaves. Red spider mite. Remove webs with damp cloth or sponge, then spray with diluted malathion, especially under leaves. Repeat every 14 days until symptoms disappear. Spray to improve humidity.

New leaves small, no flowers. Needs feeding. Feed every 14 days in growing and flowering season with houseplant food diluted to maker's recommended strength.

Leaves become crisp and pale. Air too dry. Spray twice a week in hot dry rooms with soft, tepid water, protecting flowers from spray with paper or your hand.

Leaves wrinkle and contract in winter. Soil too dry. Plant will not be harmed unless soil dries out completely: a dry period in winter helps flower production following summer.

Buds dry up. Damage by sunlight. Move into area of good, diffused light while buds are forming but out of direct sun.

Leaves curl up, flowers fall. Gas or other fumes. Move to fume-free room.

Flowers fall and no new ones appear in summer. Compost too dry. Water immediately by plunging pot into bucket of water for 10–15 minutes, then drain. Allow surface to dry out between waterings but check regularly in hot weather.

Drops of nectar on flowers. This is natural but place tray or cloth under flowers to protect furniture.

Leaves look dull. Too cold. Move to warmer room and keep above 65°F (18°C) in summer and at 50°F (10°C) in winter.

Lanky growth, no flowers appear. Too dark. Move into position in very good light. Plant will stand direct sunlight except when buds are forming, and needs full light in winter.

Jasminum polyanthum

Jasmine

This is a winter flowering plant producing hundreds of tiny white star-like flowers with an attractive scent. Often confused with *Stephanotis floribunda*, this variety of Jasmine requires quite cool conditions. It is best grown in a greenhouse or conservatory and brought into the house when in flower. When flowering is over, it should be pruned back by half to encourage it to form a compact shape the following year. In the summer, the leading shoots should be progressively pinched out every month to encourage side shoots to grow.

Light: Full diffused daylight (see p.12). Direct summer sun should be avoided as the plant will quickly dry out.

Temperature: Best at 60°F (16°C), and not more than 65°F (18°C) with good ventilation in summer, and 55°F (13°C) when flowering in winter: any hotter and the plant will turn brown. Minimum temperature at any time is 45-50°F (7-10°C).

Water: Every 4 or 5 days when in flower; 2 or 3 times a week in summer, keeping compost always moist, but not standing in water. In winter, water only when compost surface dried out, except while flowering.

Humidity: Spray daily if atmosphere dry, avoiding open flowers. Plant pot in another pot with moist peat between.

Feeding: Every 14 days in spring and summer with liquid houseplant food diluted to maker's instructions (see p.8).

Soil: 3 parts loam-based No.2 with 1 part peat added.

Repotting: In early spring when flowering finished, after pruning. Main growing tips of the foliage, which grows in spring and summer, should be pinched out monthly until end of summer.

Cleaning: Humidity spraying adequate. No leafshine.

The Jasmine is a winter-flowering plant which produces a mass of tiny, star-shaped white or pink flowers. Dry atmospheres quickly cause both flowers and foliage to shrivel, so spray daily in centrally heated rooms.

Leaves pale with webs underneath. Red spider mite. Remove webs with damp cloth or sponge, then spray with diluted malathion, especially under leaves. Repeat every 14 days until symptoms disappear. Improve humidity by standing pot on saucer of wet pebbles.

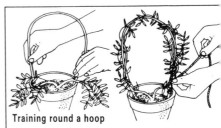

Training round a hoop

1. Push ends of wire hoop or thin cane so that they are ⅔ down pot on opposite sides. Bend plant stem to one side of hoop and gently twist around.

2. To secure plant to hoop, tie twine to one end of hoop and thread it along, looping it loosely around stem. Do not tie knots or stem may be damaged.

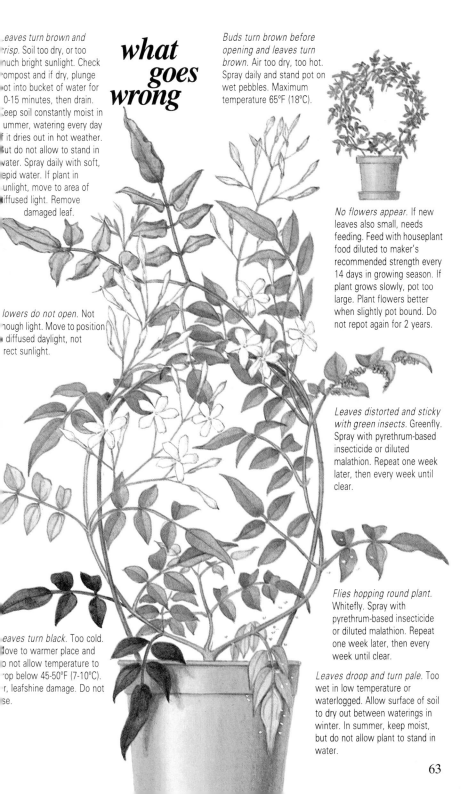

eaves turn brown and
risp. Soil too dry, or too
much bright sunlight. Check
compost and if dry, plunge
pot into bucket of water for
0-15 minutes, then drain.
Keep soil constantly moist in
summer, watering every day
if it dries out in hot weather.
But do not allow to stand in
water. Spray daily with soft,
tepid water. If plant in
sunlight, move to area of
diffused light. Remove
damaged leaf.

what goes wrong

Buds turn brown before
opening and leaves turn
brown. Air too dry, too hot.
Spray daily and stand pot on
wet pebbles. Maximum
temperature 65°F (18°C).

No flowers appear. If new
leaves also small, needs
feeding. Feed with houseplant
food diluted to maker's
recommended strength every
14 days in growing season. If
plant grows slowly, pot too
large. Plant flowers better
when slightly pot bound. Do
not repot again for 2 years.

lowers do not open. Not
nough light. Move to position
in diffused daylight, not
rect sunlight.

Leaves distorted and sticky
with green insects. Greenfly.
Spray with pyrethrum-based
insecticide or diluted
malathion. Repeat one week
later, then every week until
clear.

Flies hopping round plant.
Whitefly. Spray with
pyrethrum-based insecticide
or diluted malathion. Repeat
one week later, then every
week until clear.

eaves turn black. Too cold.
Move to warmer place and
do not allow temperature to
drop below 45-50°F (7-10°C).
r, leafshine damage. Do not
se.

Leaves droop and turn pale. Too
wet in low temperature or
waterlogged. Allow surface of soil
to dry out between waterings in
winter. In summer, keep moist,
but do not allow plant to stand in
water.

63

Lapageria rosea

Chilean bell flower

This beautiful evergreen climber produces spectacular waxy, translucent, rosy-crimson flowers which appear from late summer until late autumn. It will grow to 20ft (6m) if unpruned and can be used in the greenhouse to climb over an archway, as the flowers hang downwards. In the home, it is best trained on a trellis and kept in relatively small pots to keep the roots compact and pruned by one third after flowering. This plant is like a magnet to many of the common houseplant pests, including greenfly, which will attack young shoots in spring, thrips, mealy bug and scale insect.

The Chilean bell flower is an evergreen climber whose spectacular rosy crimson flowers hang down gracefully. If allowed to grow unchecked, it will easily reach 20ft (6m) s should be trained on a trellis and regularly pruned.

Light: Diffused daylight in summer (see p.12), avoiding direct sun. Increase light in winter, including full sun.

Temperature: Maintain 65–70°F (18–21°C) in summer, with maximum 75°F (24°C). Winter minimum 55°F (13°C).

Water: At least twice a week in summer, to keep always moist. Never allow pot to stand in water. Reduce to weekly in winter, allowing compost surface to dry out between waterings.

Humidity: Spray daily in spring and summer until flowers appear. Maintain humidity when flowering by standing pot on a saucer of pebbles almost covered with water. Do not spray in autumn or winter.

Feeding: Every 14 days in spring and summer with liquid houseplant food diluted to half maker's instructions (see p.8).

Soil: 3 parts fibrous peat, 1 part loam-based No.2 and 1 part equal quantities of charcoal and peat.

Repotting: In early spring for young plants, into pots one size larger to a maximum 7in (18cm). Then repot into same sized pot.

Cleaning: Spray with soft water. No leafshine.

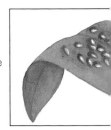

Leaves sticky with green insects. Greenfly. Spray every week with diluted malathion to prevent attack; greenfly can quickly damage this plant.

Whole plant turns black. Leafshine damage. Do not use. Clean only by carefully dusting with feather duster or camel hair brush.

Plant fails to flower. Too dark. Move into good light position. Will stand full sunlight except in summer, when it will be too hot.

Webs on flowers and leaves. Red spider mite. Remove webs with damp cloth or sponge, then spray with diluted malathion, especially under leaves. Repeat every 14 days until symptoms disappear. Improve humidity by standing pot on saucer of wet pebbles.

Discs on leaves. Scale insect. Spray underside of leaves with diluted malathion and after 48 hours remove discs with thumbnail. Repeat every week for 4 weeks until clear.

what goes wrong

New leaves small, no flowers appear. Needs feeding. Feed every week in growing and flowering season with houseplant food diluted to maker's recommended strength.

Leaves scorched. Caused by spraying in bright sunlight. Spray only in early morning or evening if plant is in full light.

Leaves eaten away. Thrips. Spray thoroughly with diluted malathion and repeat after 1 week. If in greenhouse, fumigate.

Leaves turn black and stems rot, especially in winter. Botrytis, plant too cold and damp. Spray with fungicide, then place in warmer position, at least 55°F (13°C) and spray less often. Allow compost surface to dry out between waterings in winter.

Flies hopping around plant. Whitefly. Spray with pyrethrum-based insecticide or diluted malathion. Repeat one week later, then weekly until clear.

Plant goes limp, especially in summer. Soil too dry or too much hot sunlight. Plunge pot into bucket of water for 10-15 minutes, then drain. Keep soil constantly moist in summer. Keep out of hot summer sun.

Leaves flop and dry out. Air too dry or too hot. Spray daily with soft tepid water and provide extra humidity by standing pot on saucer of damp pebbles. Best kept at 65-70°F (18-21°C) and not more than 75°F (24°C).

White cotton-wool patches here leaves join stem. Mealy bug. Spray with diluted malathion and remove bugs and 'wool' with tweezers. Repeat every 14 days until symptoms disappear. Or, paint bugs with methylated spirits and remove with tweezers.

Flower buds fall off. Too cold. Move to warmer place, at least 55°F (13°C).

Paphiopedilon

Slipper orchid

Slipper orchids look exotic but are not difficult to grow and bring into bloom. They are also still sometimes found under the name *Cypripedium*. The leaves are often hairy, the older leaves withering with age. They produce flowers on single stems from late summer onwards. As with all orchids, the compost mixture is most important since the plant requires copious amounts of water which must be able to drain through the compost almost immediately. Ordinary potting mixtures soon become waterlogged in these conditions and if this is allowed to happen, the roots will rot and the plant soon die.

Light: Diffused daylight (see p.12), avoiding midday sun.
Temperature: 65°F (18°C) minimum and 80°F (27°C) maximum in summer, 50°F (10°C) minimum in winter.
Water: 2 or 3 times weekly in summer, once a week in winter, early spring. Compost must be always moist.
Humidity: Spray every 2 days with soft, tepid water in spring and summer. Stand pot on saucer of pebbles almost covered with water. Do not spray if temperature below 55°F (13°C), when plant is in flower, or in autumn or winter.
Feeding: Weekly in growing and flowering season using liquid houseplant food diluted to maker's instructions (see p.8). Do not feed from after flowers fade until spring.
Soil: Special orchid compost, comprising 3 parts osmunda fibre to 1 part sphagnum moss. Alternatively, mix 2 parts loam-based No. 2, 1 part peat, 1 part leafmould, and one-eighth part sand and crushed lime.
Repotting: After flowering, only if pot-bound: usually every 2 years.
Cleaning: Wipe leaves with damp cloth. No leafshine.

Slipper orchids produce their beautiful flowers on single stems from late summer onwards. They are usually sold in 4in (10cm) pots and produce 2 or 3 flowers at a height of about 10in (25cm). A humid atmosphere is important in spring and summer.

Webs on leaves and flower buds. Red spider mite. Remove webs with damp cloth or sponge, then spray with diluted malathion, especially under leaves. Repeat every 14 days until symptoms disappear. Improve humidity by standing pot on saucer of wet pebbles.

Plant dries out and turns brown. Compost too dry. Plunge pot into bucket of water for 10–15 minutes, then drain. Keep constantly moist in summer, watering every day if it dries out in hot weather. Do not allow to stand in water. Spray every 2 days with soft, tepid water in spring and summer.

Leaves droop. Too wet, waterlogged. Drain away any excess water from saucer and allow surface of compost to dry out before watering again. Check compost drains freely and never leave plant standing in water.

No new growth at all. Too cold. Maintain at least 65°F (18°C) in summer and 50°F (10°C) in winter.

Flower and leaves begin to dry out although humidity sufficient. Damage by sunlight. Move into area of diffused sunlight, out of harmful rays of sun. Remove damaged leaf.

o flowers appear. Pot too rge. Plant flowers better if ightly pot bound. Do not pot again for 2 years.

lower bud dries out and hrivels. Air too hot and dry. pray every 2 days with soft pid water and provide extra umidity by standing pot on aucer of wet pebbles. Do ot allow water to remain n buds at night. Keep emperature at least 65°F 8°C) in spring and summer.

Division

1. These orchids have underground rhizomes which can be divided when plant has produced at least 6 separate groups of leaves.

2. When flowers have died, knock plant from pot. Remove stale soil, then pull or cut rhizomes apart. Each section should have both roots and leaves.

3. Pot each section separately in recommended compost with good drainage. Choose pot large enough to hold rhizome horizontally with at least 1½in (3cm) space around for new growth.

4. Spray daily with fine spray until leaves begin to show growth, then treat as normal plant.

Buds damaged at night. Thrips. Spray with diluted malathion immediately and repeat weekly for 4 weeks. When spraying with water, do not allow water to remain on flower bud at night as this will also damage buds.

what goes wrong

Plant turns black. In winter, too cold at night. Keep at temperature of at least 50°F (10°C). Or leafshine damage. Do not use. Wipe leaves with damp cloth to clean.

White cotton-wool patches around base of plant. Mealy bug. Spray with diluted malathion and remove bugs and 'wool' with tweezers. Repeat every 14 days until symptoms disappear. Or, paint bugs with methylated spirits and remove with tweezers.

Passion flower

When grown in the home, this plant is usually trained around a hoop or on a small trellis, which is how it is generally sold as a houseplant. *Passiflora* is best suited to a conservatory or porch as it requires a very cool winter temperature; it can even be grown out of doors if protected from frost. With full light it will flower freely in summer through to winter and may even produce fruit. Choose plants with many buds still unopened, not with the remains of old flowers.

Passion flowers were named by early Spanish missionaries to South America, who saw the symbols of Christ's passion in the strange form of the flowers. Different parts of the flower represent the wounds, nails, cross, crown of thorns and the apostles.

Light: Full light, including sun. If in too dark conditions it will not flower.

Temperature: Maintain 65–75°F (18–24°C) from spring to autumn, never exceeding 75°F (24°C) in summer. Maintain 55–65°F (13–18°C) from autumn to spring.

Water: Copiously every 2 days from spring to late summer to keep moist – daily if temperature goes up to 75°F (24°C). In winter water only when soil surface seems dry, i.e. every 7–10 days.

Humidity: Spray with soft water 2 or 3 times a week in summer. Do not spray in winter or when plant is in sunshine.

Feeding: Weekly in spring and summer with liquid houseplant food diluted to half maker's instructions (see p.8). Do not feed in winter.

Soil: 2 parts peat, 2 parts loam and 1 part coarse sand.

Repotting: Annually in spring after plant has been pruned by about one-third to encourage strong new growth. Pot up into one size larger pot only, or plant will produce abundant foliage and few flowers that year. (If larger plant wanted, pot up into pot 2 sizes larger. Plant may not flower that year.) Remove weak shoots altogether.

Cleaning: Humidity spraying adequate. No leafshine.

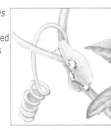

White cotton-wool patches where leaf joins stem. Mealy bug. Spray with diluted malathion and remove bugs and 'wool' with tweezers. Repeat every 14 days until symptoms disappear. Or, paint bugs with methylated spirits and remove with tweezers.

New leaves small. Needs feeding. Feed with houseplant food diluted to half maker's recommended strength every week in growing season.

Leaves distorted and sticky. Greenfly. Spray with pyrethrum-based insecticide or diluted malathion. Repeat one week later, then once a week until symptoms disappear.

Plant looks limp and leaves turn yellow. Soil too dry. Plunge pot into bucket of water for 10–15 minutes, then drain.

Whole leaves turn furry with white powder. Botrytis, mould. Too cold and damp. Spray with fungicide then place in warmer place, at least 55°F (13°C). Spray with water less often. Allow compost to dry out between waterings in winter.

Pruning

Prune in spring, before buds appear. Cut back main stem by one-third, cutting at an angle just above a leaf, using sharp secateurs. Shorten side shoots by half and cut out any weedy shoots at the base.

Fruit remains yellow, with a few black spots. Too cold. Move to warmer, lighter position, at least 65°F (18°C).

what goes wrong

Flowers have scorch marks. Caused by spraying in sunlight. Do not spray flowers and spray leaves only in early morning and evening.

Plant wilts though soil is moist. Plant waterlogged, standing in water. Drain away any water in saucer and allow surface to dry out before watering again. Then keep moist in summer but never allow pot base to stand in water. Always throw away excess that drains through after watering.

Growing tips droop and flop. Too hot and air too dry. Move to position with better ventilation and improve humidity by spraying regularly and standing pot on saucer of damp pebbles. Maximum temperature 75°F (24°C).

Leaves pale with webs underneath. Red spider mite. Remove webs with damp cloth or sponge, then spray with diluted malathion, especially under leaves. Repeat every 14 days until symptoms disappear. Improve humidity around plant.

No flowers appear. Pot too large or, if new leaves also small, needs feeding. Flowers best when slightly pot bound. Do not repot for 2 years. Feed with houseplant food diluted to half maker's recommended strength every week in the growing season. If leaves are growing rapidly, too much food. Withhold for 2–3 weeks, and always use half strength food. Do not feed in winter. If other conditions seem correct, not enough light. Move to position in very good light. Plant will stand direct sunshine.

Plumbago capensis

Cape leadwort

Said to be a remedy against lead poisoning, this plant's name is derived from the Latin *plumbum*, 'lead'. It is a climbing or trailing shrub which is usually bought growing on a wire hoop. The pale blue flowers are carried in spikes at the ends of the trailing stems. In the greenhouse it can be trained along the rafters or a wall. It should be cut back to within 6in (15cm) of pot after flowering and kept cool and drier for a rest period in the winter. Frequent watering and increased heat from the following spring will produce prolific new growth. Flowers appear on the current season's growth.

The Cape leadwort is a climbing or trailing shrub with pale blue or lavender-coloured flowers which are carried as spike on the end of the stems. The vigorous growth should be pruned hard after flowering as the flowers only appear on the current season's growth.

Light: Full light, avoiding midday sun in summer. Keep in shady situation in winter, when dormant.

Temperature: Keep at 45°F (7°C) in winter, increasing to 55–70°F (13–21°C) in early spring until autumn.

Water: Twice a week in spring and summer, keeping compost moist at all times, but pot must not stand in water. Water in winter only when compost surface has dried out, about once every 10 days.

Humidity: Spray with soft tepid water daily in spring and summer. Avoid flowers.

Feeding: Every 14 days after the first flower buds appear, with liquid fertilizer diluted to maker's instructions (see p.8). Stop feeding in autumn and winter.

Soil: Equal parts leafmould, peat, sand and loam-based No.3.

Repotting: In early spring into pot one size larger, up to maximum pot size 10in (25cm). Then repot into same size pot annually, with fresh soil. Plant grows successfully only when root ball is compact. Put plenty of broken crocks into bottom of pot.

Cleaning: Humidity spraying, out of direct sunlight, adequate. No leafshine.

White cotton-wool patches where leaf joins stem. Mealy bug. Spray with diluted malathion and remove bugs and 'wool' with tweezers. Repeat every 14 days until symptoms disappear. Or, paint bugs with methylated spirits and remove with tweezers. When spraying, avoid flowers and buds.

Leaves black when temperature and humidity correct. Leafshine damage. Do not use. Clean only by spraying with soft, tepid water. Remove damaged leaf.

Leaves shrivel. May be too cold, too wet or too dry. Check temperature. If less than 55°F (13°C) in summer or 45°F (7°C) in winter and compost feels moist, plant too cold. Move to warmer place. If temperature correct in winter, too wet. Allow surface to dry out between watering in winter. If temperature correct in summer, soil too dry. Plunge pot into bucket of water for 10-15 minutes, then dr

Few flowers in spring and summer. Should have been pruned previous year. Prune current season's flower stems when flowering finished to encourage new growth on which next year's flowers form. Do not prune in spring before flowering.

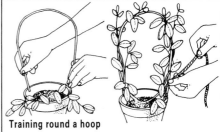

Training round a hoop
1. Push ends of wire hoop or thin cane so that they are ⅔ down pot on opposite sides. Bend plant stem to one side of hoop and gently twist around.

2. To secure plant to hoop, tie twine to one end of hoop and thread it along, looping it loosely around stem. Do not tie knots or stem may be damaged.

what goes wrong

Flower buds do not open. Too cold and too dark. Move to warmer place, at least 65°F (18°C) in summer, 70°F (21°C) if possible. Make sure plant is in good light.

New leaves small. Needs feeding. Feed with houseplant food diluted to maker's recommended strength every 14 days after first flower buds appear.

Flower buds covered with sticky green insects. Greenfly. Spray with pyrethrum-based insecticide or diluted malathion. Repeat one week later, then every week until clear.

Leaves turn brown and crisp, flower buds drop. Too hot and air too dry. Move to cooler place (less than 70°F, 21°C) if possible, with good ventilation. Spray with soft, tepid water and improve humidity by standing pot on saucer of wet pebbles.

Lower leaves rot. Waterlogged, plant standing in water. Happens especially in winter. Drain away any water in saucer and allow surface of compost to dry out before watering again. Then keep moist in summer but allow surface to dry out between waterings in winter. Always throw away excess water that drains through pot into saucer after watering.

Trailing velvet plant

Named after Jean de la Ruelle who was botanist and physician to Francis I of France in the early 16th century, these free-flowering plants were fairly common in Victorian times but had all but disappeared from flower shops until quite recently. Attractive both for the beauty of their flowers and their silvery veined leaves, they are now coming back into favour. Watch especially for greenfly which attack the tender growing tips of the stems.

The trailing velvet plant flowers in winter but its silver-veined leaves make it attractive all year round. To prolong its flowering period, use artificial lighting to give more 'daylight' hours in winter.

Light: Full diffused, not direct sun. In winter give 8 hours light, using artificial lighting (p.12) to prolong flowering.
Temperature: At least 55°F (13°F) and in summer between 55 and 65°F (13–18°C). Maximum 70°F (21°C) for short periods if humidity high.
Water: From early spring for 6 weeks water as compost is about to dry out (every 10 days). Otherwise 2 days after surface feels dry (every 5 days).
Humidity: High if temperature over 65°F (18°C). Spray twice weekly with soft water when 55–65°F (13–18°C), daily if higher. Stand pot on saucer of wet pebbles all year round. Do not spray in rest period. Do not spray flowers.
Feeding: Fortnightly except during rest period. Dilute houseplant food to maker's recommended strength.
Repotting: In early autumn. After 2 years take cuttings in summer and root in peat/sand mixture. Pot up after 12 weeks in normal compost and feed.
Soil: Loam-based No. 2 mixed in equal parts with moss.
Cleaning: Humidity spray adequate. Use only soft water. Do not use leafshine.

White powdery mould on leaves and stems. Botrytis, plant too cold and damp. Spray with fungicide, then place in warmer position and spray with water less often. Allow compost surface to dry out between waterings. Minimum temperature 55°F (13°C). Remove damaged leaves.

Spotty burn marks on flowers and leaves. Caused by spraying in bright sunlight. Move into area of diffused light and remove damaged leaf or flower.

Humidity
Stand pot on saucer of pebbles half covered in water all year round. Do not allow pot base to stand in water. If temperature over 65°F (18°C) provide higher humidity by daily spraying. Do not spray in spring rest period. Protect flowers from spray.

Insects cover tender growing tips. Greenfly. Spray with pyrethrum-based insecticide or diluted malathion. Repeat one week later and every week until clear.

what goes wrong

Flies hopping round plant. Whitefly. Spray with pyrethrum-based insecticide or diluted malathion. Repeat one week later and every week until clear.

Whole plant goes limp though temperature correct. Waterlogged, standing in water. Drain away any water in saucer and allow surface of compost to dry out before watering again. Then keep moist but never allow pot base to stand in water. Always throw away excess that drains through after watering.

Flowers rot though temperature and humidity correct. Flowers sprayed with water. Protect with your hand or paper when mist spraying leaves.

aves turn black. Too cold leafshine damage. Move warmer place, at least °F (13°C). Do not use fshine. Clean only by aying with soft tepid ter. Remove damaged f.

nt straggly with no ves on lower stems. Too . Take cuttings in summer replace ageing plants.

Plant shrivels. Too dry or too hot. Check compost, and water immediately if dry by plunging pot into bucket of water and leaving for 10–15 minutes. Do not allow compost to dry out completely watering 2 days after compost surface appears dry, except in spring rest period. If over 70°F (21°C), move to cooler position.

Webs under leaves, leaves pale. Red spider mite. Remove webs with damp cloth or sponge, then spray with diluted malathion, especially under leaves. Repeat every 14 days until symptoms disappear. Improve humidity by standing pot on saucer of wet pebbles.

Plant grows lanky with no flowers. Too dark. Move to position in diffused light, not in direct sun.

Saintpaulia ionantha

African violet

The original species of this plant, found in the mountains of East Africa, was blue; it has been hybridised to produce plants which do not drop their flowers so quickly and come in a range of colours, including pink, red, white and bi-colour varieties, and with single and double flowers. A relatively small pot, warmth and high humidity are all necessary for good flower production; a pinch of Epsom salts added once to the water in early summer will encourage the plant to flower.

Light: Full light in summer, avoiding spring and summer sun. Will tolerate winter sunshine.

Temperature: Maintain 60°F (16°C) all year. Tolerates a minimum 55°F (13°C) and a maximum of 80°F (27°C) if humidity is high.

Water: Stand pot in a saucer and fill saucer to brim twice a week all year. After half an hour, tip out excess, as pot must not stand in water. Do not water top of pot.

Humidity: Do not spray. Achieve essential high humidity by standing pot on saucer of pebbles almost covered with water. Remove to another saucer for watering. Alternatively, put pot into another pot with damp peat between.

Feeding: Add liquid houseplant food every 2 weeks in spring and summer to water used for watering. Throw away excess. Use maker's recommended strength.

Soil: Peat-based potting compost.

Repotting: About every 2 years, only when plant looks really overcrowded in pot. Use shallow pots. Maintain overall rosette of leaves by removing leaves pointing towards centre of plant whenever necessary.

Cleaning: Dust with camel hair brush. No spraying, no leafshine. Remove dead flowers.

The African violet is one of the world's most popular houseplants, yet it is often reluctant to flower. Warmth is the principal secret (60°F, 16°C all year round) coupled with a special watering technique and high humidity.

Leaves turn pale. Too much light or needs feeding. If in sun, move to position in diffused light. If new leaves also small, feed. Use liquid houseplant food at recommended strength every 2 weeks in the growing season and when in flower.

Leaves turn black. Leafshine damage. Never spray with leafshine or water. If dusty, remove by carefully brushing leaves with soft camel-hair brush.

New leaves small and very crowded. Needs repotting. Repot in spring into next size pot, but keep pot bound.

Watering

Water twice weekly all year round. Stand pot in saucer and fill saucer to brim with water. Leave for half an hour, then drain away excess. Do not leave standing in water.

Humidity

Plant needs high humidity but must not be sprayed. Put pebbles in saucer and stand pot on top. Add water to saucer until it is half way up pebbles. Do not let bottom of pot touch water.

Healthy plant does not flower. Pot too large. Plant flowers better when slightly pot bound. Do not repot for 2 years.

No flowers but plant in correct sized pot and in correct conditions. Add pinch of Epsom salts to water once only to trigger flowering season.

Flowers small and sparse. Usually occurs if second flush of flowers in same season. Remove faded flowers and feed every 2 weeks throughout summer with houseplant food at recommended strength.

Flowers have translucent marks. Water damage. Do not allow water to get on flowers. Plant needs humid atmosphere but do not spray.

what goes wrong

Leaves and flowers rot. Too frequent watering and watering from top. Water twice a week all year round by standing pot in saucer of water for half an hour. Do not water from above. Discard water after half an hour.

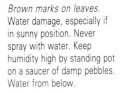

Brown marks on leaves. Water damage, especially if in sunny position. Never spray with water. Keep humidity high by standing pot on a saucer of damp pebbles. Water from below.

Healthy plant suddenly turns yellow. Gas fumes or cold draughts. Move to protected position in fume-free room.

Leaves curl or look limp and dry. Needs watering or too hot and air too dry. Water twice a week all year round, always from below. If temperatures near 80°F (27°C) improve humidity by standing on saucer of damp pebbles. Do not spray.

Leaves look limp and weedy. Too cold. Move to warmer place. Do not allow temperature to drop below 55°F (13°C).

75

Cape primrose

This plant's exotic-looking flowers stand high above large, rather incongruous, bright green, somewhat distorted leaves. The leaves are very brittle, so great care needs to be taken of the plant in the home. The commonest flower colour is blue, but white and red varieties are available occasionally. Propagation is unusual: a leaf is cut along the length of the centre vein with a sharp knife and the leaf put in sharp sand with the exposed vein just buried along its length. With bottom heat, plantlets will grow along the leaf. In low light levels, a sheet of tinfoil put between the top of the pot and the leaves will reflect light on the underside of the leaves, greatly helping culture.

The Cape primrose's lush green leaves are rather few in number but in summer set off well the delicate blue flowers. White and red varieties are also available. When buying, look carefully for damaged leaves as they are brittle and break easily.

Light: Full light, avoiding midday sun.
Temperature: 65–70°F (18–21°C) all summer, with maximum 75°F (24°C). Winter minimum 60°F (16°C).
Water: 2 or 3 times a week with soft tepid water to keep moist in summer, but plant must not stand in water. In winter, water when compost surface is dried out: about once a week.
Humidity: Must be high. Spray twice a week in spring and summer when not in flower. When in flower, stand pot on saucer of pebbles almost covered with water, or put pot into an outer pot with moist peat between.
Feeding: Monthly in spring and summer with liquid food diluted to half maker's instructions (see p.8).
Soil: 4 parts peat-based potting compost to 1 part sharp sand.
Repotting: Annually in spring up to maximum pot size 4in (10cm); in effect, after second year, use same pot with fresh soil.
Cleaning: Carefully brush leaves with camel-hair paint brush. No leafshine.

what goes wrong

Leaves turn black. Too cold. Move to warmer place, at least 60°F (16°C). Or leafshine damage. Do not use. Clean by dusting carefully with feather duster or camel hair brush.

Leaves sticky. Greenfly. Spray with pyrethrum-based insecticide or diluted malathion. Repeat one week later, then every week until clear.

Leaves shrivel, flowers fall off. Compost too dry. Water immediately and keep always moist but not waterlogged in summer. In winter, water only once a week, allowing surface to begin to dry out.

Leaf propagation

1. Cut down centre of main vein and dip cut surface in hormone rooting powder.

2. Place in tray of sharp sand with cut vein just covered. Keep warm (60°F, 16°C) and moist. New plantlets grow along vein.

Plant looks limp. Cold draughts or smoke affected. Move to protected position in fume-free room.

Leaves pale, no flowers. Not enough light. Move to position in good light. Plant will stand sunlight except at midday.

Flies hopping round compost surface. Whitefly. Spray with pyrethrum-based insecticide or diluted malathion. Repeat one week later.

Leaves very large, no flowers. Too much food and pot too large. Do not repot for 2 years. Reduce feeding to half maker's recommended strength, once a month only.

Leaves turn brown, flowers fall. Too hot. Move to cooler place with more ventilation. Spray daily with soft, tepid water. Maximum temperature 75°F (24°C).

One or two leaves rot at base. Waterlogged, standing in water. Drain away any water in saucer and allow compost to dry out on surface before watering again. Water only once a week in winter. Never stand pot in water.

Leaves and flower stems rot away. Botrytis. Too cold and damp. Spray with fungicide, then place in warmer room and spray less often. Allow surface to just dry out between watering in winter and keep at least 60°F (16°C). Remove damaged leaves at compost level.

Blue flowered torch

A member of the Bromeliad family, the Blue flowered torch originates in Peru, where it grows on tree branches. The foliage is rather uninteresting and somewhat messy, but the spathe, formed of a series of spear-shaped carmine-coloured bracts, will suddenly produce, one after the other, deep blue, exotic-looking flowers with a white spotted throat. These gorgeous flowers are a splendid reward for having to live with an otherwise untidy specimen. Propagation is by potting up offsets in spring after the parent plant has died. The life cycle is three years from offset to flowering.

The Blue flowered torch has a rather messy looking mass of foliage but its broad bract produces purple flowers which are quite outstanding in their colour density. Like other bromeliads it flowers only once in its life cycle but new plants can be grown from its offsets.

Light: Full light, including sunlight. Will survive happily in indirect daylight if it is reasonably bright.

Temperature: Best between 70 and 75°F (21–24°C) though will grow in summer temperatures as low as 65°F (18°C). Minimum winter temperature 55°F (13°C).

Water: Twice weekly in summer to keep moist, pouring water into centre of plant and allowing it to trickle into compost. In winter, water only when surface has dried out, about once every week to 10 days.

Humidity: Spray daily with soft water in spring and summer, not in autumn or winter.

Feeding: Every 14 days in summer only with liquid houseplant food diluted to half maker's instructions (see p.8).

Soil: 4 parts peat-based potting compost to 1 part chopped sphagnum moss.

Repotting: Pot up offset in spring and repot after 1 year. Do not repot in second year. Plant has very small roots, just enough to hold it upright.

Cleaning: Humidity spraying adequate. No leafshine. Remove unsightly brown tips with sharp scissors.

Offsets

1. When parent plant dies and offset is about half its size, remove offset and its roots from parent with sharp knife.

2. Pot in new pot, firming compost around base. Water well and keep pot covered with polythene for 2–3 days to provide extra humidity.

Plant rots. Botrytis, plant too cold and damp. Spray with fungicide, then place in warmer atmosphere, best around 70–75°F (21–24°C) but never below 55°F (13°C). Do not spray until plant begins to recover and allow surface of compost to dry out between waterings.